The
Modern
Art of
War

The Modern Art of War

Sun Tzu's Hidden Path to Peace and Wholeness

Hunter Liguore

WATKINS
1893

This edition first published in the UK and USA in 2024 by
Watkins, an imprint of Watkins Media Limited
Unit 11, Shepperton House
89-93 Shepperton Road
London
N1 3DF

enquiries@watkinspublishing.com

Design and typography copyright © Watkins Media Limited 2024

Text copyright © Hunter Liguore 2024

Hunter Liguore has asserted her right under the Copyright, Designs
and Patents Act 1988 to be identified as the author of this work.

1 2 3 4 5 6 7 8 9 10

Typeset by JCS Publishing Services Ltd

Printed and bound in The United Kingdom

A CIP record for this book is available from the British Library

ISBN: 978-1-78678-845-0 (Paperback
ISBN: 978-1-78678-851-1 (eBook)

www.watkinspublishing.com

"To fight and conquer consists of breaking the
Mind's resistance without fighting."

– Sun Tzu

CONTENTS

GETTING STARTED

SUN TZU'S HIDDEN PATH TO PEACE AND WHOLENESS

"The first and best of victories, the lowest and worst of defeats, which each person gains or sustains at the hands, not of another, but of himself, shows that there is a war against ourselves going on within every one of us."

— Plato, *Laws*, Book I, 626:e

From the time Sun Tzu's *Art of War*[1] was first translated in 1782 by the Jesuit priest Joseph Amiot, it has been received by the Western world as a military treatise and a tactical how-to guide for waging war on a battlefield. It has served military strategists for the last 2,600 years, all the way through to modern times, where business managers and other professionals have used its tactics against competitors.

But what if the book had a different purpose and was never intended for generals or CEOs, but really for the common, everyday person seeking greater meaning in their life?

§

Contrary to the customary view, Sun Tzu was hardly a military general, but a spiritual advisor, a mystic or sage, who authored an inspired treatise on matters related to the war going on in the mind, and used the commonness of military combat—prevalent at the time it was written— as a symbolic allegory to talk about it. Likewise, the treatise, though thoroughly misrepresented throughout history, wasn't written for a king but for the common people, its message simple: *the Hidden Path to Peace and Wholeness*.

---

1   Also translated as *The Right Way of War*.

No authorship was ascribed to *Art of War*, for to do so would be to suggest there was still an "I" or Self present. Instead, what was passed on to the modern age by historians as *Art of War*, written by "Sun Tzu," follows the tradition of philosophical teachers like Lao Tzu, Homer, or Vyasa, author of the *Bhagavad Gita*. Even to suggest Sun Tzu was male would be to impose an identity on this unknown author. In keeping with the tradition of symbolic authorship, and to encourage the idea that we're all Master Suns, this book will refer to Sun Tzu as *she/he/they* interchangeably, to not only support Sun Tzu's inclusive teaching, but to further dismantle preconceived notions of this unknown teacher.

The Modern Art of War: Sun Tzu's Hidden Path to Peace and Wholeness offers readers a new interpretation of Sun Tzu's *Art of War*, one that explores the ancient wisdom of self-discovery through the truest art of war: the fight to control your mind and the thoughts that rule it. These lessons come with a unique set of tools and exercises that can be applied in a gradual progression of steps that when mastered, can ultimately guide the average person to live an abundant life through inner peace.

The book, as a whole, is an invitation—an opportunity—to conquer the enemies threatening the kingdom of inner peace. When we attain serenity, our natural state, our life takes on new meaning. We can begin to live with greater harmony, kindness, unity, and equanimity,[2] which trickles into everything we do, making our life, and subsequently our world, a more harmonious place.

That's the *hidden* message of *Art of War*.

This gentle wisdom, as originally intended by Sun Tzu, has been rewritten in its entirety and presented as a new work in these pages.

THE ORIGINS OF THE SUN TZU MYTH

To get you started, it's important to know that Sun Tzu belonged to a family of military experts, or a family guild, that reported to Ho Lu, king of the Wu province in China, sometime in the 5th century BCE. Impressed by the many battles won, Ho Lu appointed Sun Tzu as the General to his army and, as the story goes, Sun Tzu later composed the treatise *Art of War* after years of continued military success.

---

2   Equanimity, as offered by Sun Tzu, is cultivated as an experience of Wholeness, in which the mind is not experiencing shifting emotions but emanating calm, united with harmony and perfection.

What may not be readily known is that each family guild *owned* the military information or skill they'd specialized in—in this case, war tactics and strategies—and then passed this knowledge on *only* to their descendants, usually orally and through practice, similar to the medieval blacksmith training their kin to meld iron in a specific, time-honored way.

Why then, if Sun Tzu's war strategies were owned and highly valuable—*even guarded*—by the family guild, would Sun Tzu write them down, essentially giving away the family secrets?

If we regard the guild as constituting job security, then to share information would be to give the competition the advantage, severely reducing their ability to survive long-term. As the army's general, if Sun Tzu *had* shared her leading war strategies, then it would have hindered her own advancement, ruined her reputation, and even made her replaceable.

Equally, if King Ho Lu *had* truly commissioned Sun Tzu to create the ultimate battlefield workbook to make him a great ruler, able to conquer vast lands, then he would have rewarded Sun Tzu with enormous wealth and a healthy legacy, including lands and a title. Additionally, Sun Tzu's successes might've then been recorded in greater detail, similar to that of other historically celebrated and remembered military generals, such as Miyamoto Musashi, known for *The Book of Five Rings*.

If Sun Tzu was such an acclaimed general, why aren't there more records of his winnings and legacy?

If, however, Sun Tzu *wasn't* a general but a mystic, in the tradition of other philosophical masters, then the information would have been written and preserved by her students, able to interpret the hidden wisdom with one purpose: to alleviate the suffering of human existence through the practice of taming the disquieted mind.

Over time, as the Sun Tzu lineage and school died out, its understanding was lost to the majority of people, until rediscovered, only to be misread—until now.

CENTURIES OF MISINTERPRETATION

Sun Tzu's *Art of War* is certainly not the only Inspired Wisdom that has been misinterpreted throughout the ages. Coded philosophical texts have existed for centuries in human history, many of which have been reduced to a surface story or flourished only as a myth (thus deemed untrue), leaving the deeper, between-the-lines interpretation to be abandoned or lost.[3] But how does the originally intended meaning get overlooked in the first place and why hide it?

One idea is that most sacred texts contain two interpretations: one moral and one philosophical (Inspired Wisdom). Generally-speaking, the moral story is right at the surface (exoteric) and easily understood by the reader, as it focuses on the ethics and virtues essential to daily life. Usually, the reader stops at this interpretation, though, if given more thorough examination, a secondary, allegorical, hidden message (esoteric) can be discovered, and usually engages the knowledge of human origins and existence.

It is likely that those who'd originally heard *Art of War* had a more profound understanding of its meaning, one that went beyond physical wars and battles to its hidden strategies to conquer the disquieted mind, to win victory through self-mastery, whereby inward peace can prevail.[4] Over time, as people migrate or are conquered, new ideas come and go, and the original practices can get lost or misinterpreted in the process. When rediscovered, they're not always read with any foreknowledge of their purpose or understanding of the philosophical context in which they'd been originally written.

Both interpretations (esoteric, exoteric) have meaning and importance, while serving two different types of students: the beginning seeker and students who've made a heartfelt commitment to advance on the particular path and teaching. Teachers of Inspired Wisdom,[5] like Sun Tzu, recognized and understood the human struggle that exists in uncovering the path toward unlimited potential available to *everyone*. But rather than give both types of students *all* of the information at once, which could be counterproductive or misused, they introduced a series of steps to make the work manageable, to ensure victory.

Sun Tzu explains why this is important in the opening chapter, *Laying Plans*:

Knowing beforehand what challenges are to come will turn the weak student away.

---

3   A few examples of coded, philosophical texts include: *Beowulf, The Mabinogion,* Plato's *Laws, The Popol Vuh,* and *The Odyssey.*
4   In example, early Celtic peoples, familiar with the stories that now comprise *The Mabinogion,* may've understood the opening sentence, "Pwyll Prince of Dyved was lord of the seven Cantrevs of Dyved," to mean, "Wisdom was lord over the seven territories [of the mind]," despite its epic tone and qualities. See *Forests of Annwn* by the author.
5   Examples of teachers of Inspired Wisdom include Pythagoras and the ancient Egyptian pharaoh Ikhnaton, the latter is often misrepresented as a worshiper of the Sun Disk, which could be more accurately understood as being a symbol for mastery over ordinary consciousness.

By organizing and concealing the teaching as a progression of steps, it also allowed students to learn, practice, and master the material without being easily deterred by challenges and failure—or to give up and quit altogether. In mathematics, a student wouldn't begin calculus before learning to add and subtract. So too, a student of Sun Tzu's would approach the practice of Wholeness in a methodical way, to encourage their success over the long-term.

Likewise, hiding the inspired teachings preserved its purity, especially for those students who made a sincere commitment and held the teaching as sacred and valuable—a treasure—for the gift it would ultimately bring, witnessed through the experienced master teacher.

It goes without saying that it also kept the text from being destroyed or altered by an opposing religion, culture, or political attitude, as was nearly the case for Art of War. It only survived because its subtle spiritual truths had been disguised as a war treatise and shared among the growing military class. Since it was not deemed a religious text, it avoided being burned alongside other sacred books during a government-sanctioned purging.[6]

SUN TZU, THE MASTER SUN

It is valuable to know that Sun Tzu's story is shrouded in allegory, providing further evidence of Art of War's inspired and philosophical value over a military one. She was born with the name Sun Wu, meaning *sun war*, and later took the title of Sun Tzu or Master Sun. In Art of War, to be master of the sun is to be one who is self-aware, or one who walks in oneness with Constant-Awareness, along the Hidden Path to Peace and Wholeness:

> Traveling the highest mountain peak
> above the clouds
> beyond the earth realm
> and shrouded mysteries of the moon
> ascending to the sun.[7]

---

6   For more, see: Warring States period, under the rule of Ch'in Shih Huang-ti.
7   In various cultures, like the ancient Egyptians, Mayans, Greeks, etc., the sun has been used as an allegorical symbol for Wholeness (e.g., conscious unity, enlightenment, non-duality, union with God/Goddess/Divinity).

To be a Master Sun implies to the student that they can also overcome ordinary existence by winning mastery over their own mind.

As legend explains, the Master Sun was in the employ of Ho Lu of the Wu province—wu meaning war. Though Ho Lu is a historical person, he's used in the Sun Tzu myth to create familiarity with the contemporary listener to allegorically convey to the student that the *sun* must battle the *warring mind* to ascend earthly perception. Historically, the era that preceded Ho Lu's reign was called "the state of the Sun," which ushered in a treaty that gave a reprieve from war for several hundred years.

One might argue that even the time in which Sun Tzu was recorded to have been born was also part of the allegory: the "state of the Sun" symbolizes the perfect state or union with the Source of All Things, which (figuratively) descends into the human body (or material consciousness) of delusion, as represented by the rule of the Ho Lu state of Wu (or war).

Adding to the mythological nature of Sun Tzu, there is a well-known story about how Sun Tzu impressed Ho Lu and gained an appointment as his chief military strategist. After hearing of Sun Tzu's talent, King Lu asked the master to submit to a test: if Sun Tzu could train the female servants in the art of war, then the king would make her commander of his army.[8]

Sun Tzu agreed, then appointed two female servants as leaders of a larger faction of women "soldiers." He commanded the leaders to turn right, then left, front, and back. But the women simply giggled. Sun Tzu reportedly said, "If the commands and orders are *not* clearly given and understood, then the *General* is to blame." He tried again, only to have the same result.

Sun Tzu said, "If the commands and orders *are* clearly given and understood, then the *soldier* is to blame." With that, Sun Tzu beheaded the two female servants.

He wasn't finished. Next, Sun Tzu appointed two more female leaders and began to execute his orders, which were followed to the letter! King Lu, seeing the soldier-women disciplined and ready for battle in such a short time, appointed Sun Tzu as the General of his armies.

The story, more fable than historic fact, propelled the reputation of Sun Tzu into the memory of military leaders across history. Yet, at the heart of this gentle text lies the battle not for physical war, but war for a united and free kingdom within the mind.

---

8   This story originates from the Yin-ch'ueh-shan Han bamboo strips archaeology discovery, 1985. It was also depicted visually in *The Art of War*, dir. Padrusch, David W. (NY: A & E Home Video) 2009.

Beneath this literal story is the secret knowledge of attaining conscious-awareness—or more simply, to engage self-awareness or mastery as a constant state. It suggests peeling away the veil of a dually-perceived existence, to recognize one that's ever-present and Whole. Once revealed, we're given greater power to sustain our natural state of mental balance, free of stress, worry, doubt, fear, in favor of balanced living through joy and unity, since we are no longer seesawing between two states of consciousness or various emotions. Instead, we maintain and dwell in a state of constant balance, the ultimate freedom.

If we apply this idea to the female servant's story, we can see that Sun Tzu didn't *literally* behead the female servants, but instead cut off the root of the dual ego, thereby delivering the foundation of discipline from which self-mastery of Wholeness is attainable. In doing so, it put Sun Tzu (the Master Sun) in charge of *all the armies* (senses), in the *warring land* (the mind). With her steadfast *orders and direction* (volition), the *land* (intuition) was at *peace* (Wholeness).

SYMBOLISM IN SUN TZU'S WORK

As many books exist today that expound on the military (or surface) meaning of Sun Tzu's work, and hold a distinct purpose in world history, in the *Modern Art of War*, I will only be concerned with exploring the timeless, long-hidden (esoteric), philosophical wisdom that Sun Tzu's treatise provides, far from earthly battles to win earthly success and riches, but rather one with far greater importance: the control of one's mind.

What makes *Modern Art of War* special is that it's unconnected to any one tradition or dogma, and therefore it does not come with the limitations of separatism, providing instead, inclusion and accessibility. All are welcome here. This teaching is for the student of any origin, at any level, from any walk of life, to guide and instruct, and to offer support along the life path of self-discovery.

Because of this freedom, we can live more freely and directly engage our greatest need: to trust our hidden teacher (or warrior) to embrace a peaceful life, exactly where we are. Even if you have failed a hundred times before, Sun Tzu offers you an unadulterated space to *be*, in order to reconnect and discover the hidden part of you—like a warrior—that is 100 percent beautiful.

Going forward, as we engage the thirteen chapters, we'll uncover the meaning behind the basic codes or symbols Sun Tzu used to talk about the disquieted mind. In doing so, you will then be able to discern what is most valuable to you, and what to apply directly to your life. In this way, the book can be reread over a lifetime: as you change and grow, you'll discover one meaning one day, and then read the same passage again, years later, and it may have another meaning.

Teachers like Sun Tzu sought to guide and assist based on their own individual experience, but it's still very much the student's path to master—one that is distinct, though often inevitably shared by others.

To start there are quite a few symbols that need an interpretation that will serve you while reading. As Sun Tzu is using the world of military strategy to explore the mind and consciousness, we can view the secondary meaning behind the words to mean:

- **The State:** The Self as a whole or union of consciousness.

- **War:** The conflict between the Lower Self and the Higher Self; also the practice of observation.

- **Battlefield:** The terrain of the mind.

- **The Enemy:** The disquieted mind or conscious thoughts, emotions, perceptions; the ego that perceives the material world as *real* or unchanging. It's what will keep the student from finding their Inner Sun. It more often suggests one's conscious Self that would keep the intuitive (or Higher) Self from attaining freedom, and can be broken down into desires and earthly concerns.

- **The General:** The student on the path; one's ability to discern and act. (*Note that we don't begin the journey as a foot soldier, but as a general in command; this is very important and suggests our daily life and pursuits are in our capable hands.)

- **The Army:** The mind's defense warriors, like conscious-awareness or intuition (Intuitive-Unfolding) that wage battle in the material realm against its "enemies" (thoughts, emotions, perceptions).

- **Plans:** The Gentle-Way or path to succeed in bringing harmony to the misled perception or the Lower and Higher Self.

- **Heaven:** Yin, or Higher Consciousness.

- **Earth:** Yang, or Lower Consciousness.

THE MANY FACES OF WAR

Since *Art of War* didn't get handed down to us as *Art of Peace,* readers of this book are asked to reconsider and broaden their definition of war, to include the many facets of conflict that Sun Tzu might have intended. As you now know, the subject of war is used metaphorically for waging battle on our distracted minds. However, it's also important to consider the less obvious ways we create conflict through thought and action in our lives on a regular basis.

If asked to draw a picture of war, you might produce a mushroom-shaped cloud wreaking havoc over an unsuspecting city; there might be bloodshed, bullets, ruins and many deceased people—or people fighting with guns, tanks, drones, or even cyber-war, each side believing it is the winning side. This is physical war on a grand scale. However, when we're shown and taught what war looks like, we can miss the subtlety of it pervading other, closer places in our lives.

War—as it relates to the mind—occurs when our thoughts create division wherever we go. If we discriminate between good and bad or happy and sad, or are indifferent, we're creating a divide between ourselves and *something else.*

If we create resistance toward others in any capacity, we're engaging in a mental war.

When we venture from a state of mental balance to one of force, judgment, control, or even impose our own will upon others without consideration or consent, then we're creating mini-wars.

Consider the role our thoughts play when we stand our ground between our beliefs and someone else's, rather than respecting and valuing differences. Sometimes, we create borders and boundaries that declare we're right and another person is wrong, or less, or unequal.

Our creation of mental fences (boundaries) become the battlefield of the mind that Sun Tzu's work addresses.

Other examples include:

- An impatient driver, with flared temper and up-turned hands, cut off unexpectedly, angry.

- Arguments with others over our beliefs as we become self-righteous, unable to reconcile.

- Disagreements with neighbors or community over the things we don't like, believing our way is the *only* way.

- At the store checkout an item is rung up for a higher price and we take the error out on the staff.

- Gardeners pick weeds, creating a battle between what belongs and what doesn't—yet the Earth sees only plants.

War can be found in our criticisms, judgments, and anger, or other emotional states like envy, depression, sadness, worry. Discrimination, hate, and separatism all precipitate the thought of otherness, which in turn creates a future of conflict.

Equally, we can look in the mirror and judge ourselves critically (e.g., ugly, pretty, skinny, overweight), creating resistance to our inherent beauty. Year after year, our mind and its thoughts trick us into believing our reality is always in a seesawing state, controlling and dictating an uncertain future, and that we have no control over it.

But we do, at least according to Sun Tzu.

As soon as we begin to apply the teachings on the Hidden Path to Peace and Wholeness, we will see that it's not *others* ruining our life, the environment, or making the world a terrible place, but rather, it's in our control to immediately employ change through a quiet, peaceful mind. Then, very quickly, the people and places—our own mind—are no longer our opponents.

This unique retelling is a roadmap leading to the discovery of our innate ability to *reclaim* rulership and mastery over our consciousness (or everyday circumstances), to achieve peace between the warring states of the two perceptions or Selves (Higher and Lower Consciousness). As Wholeness becomes our natural state, we perceive our world without boundaries, since the mind becomes silent and eternal, like an all-seeing eye, symbolized in ancient Greek wisdom as Cyclops. Usually depicted as being blinded, Cyclops signifies the fall into delusion or blindness to one's whole, singular Self.

This state of non-war or peace is present and aware. Socrates, a teacher of Inspired Wisdom, explained it by saying, "I know that I know nothing." Written by Plato, many interpret the passage to show Socrates' humility, but it's actually expressing the experience of conscious-unity (or non-duality): to "know" is to be self-aware, to dwell in a state of accord with one's intuitive Wholeness, rather than relying on the thinking-mind controlled by emotional states.

In short, when the mind no longer chatters, it flows in a state of equanimity, or peace, and is present, so can't (technically) "know" anything, nor can it wield judgment or separation. Imagine what an hour of clarity and spaciousness, without the interruption of thought, might feel like. It is very powerful and yet gentle, uncoiling a state of quietude and peace that allows us to directly tap into our unquestionable wisdom, truth, and knowledge, which we may not have known previously.

Ancient Greek wisdom also depicts the non-warring mind as a *demigod*, such as Hercules, who was born with both god and human abilities. Symbolically, we're also born demigods, possessing both a divine consciousness and a material-world one (or Heaven and Earth, Yin and Yang) that grant us power (symbolized by Hercules' physical strength) over matter/creation. The material (or conscious) mind believes it's in control, limited from recognizing the divine nature that's always there, ever-seeking to *realize* this perfection.

Sun Tzu teaches that Wholeness is won through effortless-allowing— meaning, the state when we no longer resist our true nature and become all-powerful, like Hercules, honoring both our human and divine Self in balance. We don't need to fight anything. We get an intuitive nudge and actually trust it, rather than ignoring it, and begin to live in flow. At the same time, our thoughts need not be purged or forcibly stopped. In a way, it's a disservice to conceive the disquieted mind as something to be rid of. Instead, it's a tool, an "eye" that's seeing, interpreting, and guiding us gently on the matter–conscious plane, and can be harnessed to serve our intuition, rather than be at war with it.

When we cease fighting, as Sun Tzu explains, we essentially trust our knowing, and allow ourselves to be our *truest expression*, unimpeded by *anything*.

THE IMPORTANCE OF SUN TZU TODAY

As *Art of War* came to popularity during the Warring States period, a time when a majority of the public was part of the immense military complex, it was a matter of life and death to protect it. It was a selfless act that the unknown author preserved it, all for the sole purpose of benefiting and freeing others from the cycle of human suffering.

If you consider the soldiers, leaders, and common people, among others, working in and around the military class, who would have had access to it, therein lies another substantial reason for it: if you could show those fighting the actual wars that there was more to life than killing *enemies* on the battlefield—resulting in immense suffering inflicted to both sides—and instead gave them *freedom* through sacred knowledge of the path to inward peace, *you could end physical war.*

Those peaceful heroes who transcribed and preserved *Art of War* attempted to challenge the prevailing mindset of their day, which dictated the only way to establish peaceful relations was through waging physical war—yet through Sun Tzu's understanding of Wholeness, we can learn from the past, knowing, *what hurts one, hurts us all.*

Under this scope, Sun Tzu's teachings can be elevated from a text that once perpetuated war to one that offers a future where peace is visible and *living*, available to all people.

We'll never know how many *did* hear Sun Tzu's teaching and put down arms throughout history. Today, we join those committed to the Master Sun lineage of peace. We are not islands when we think. As creators, our thoughts generate a subtle vibration felt and received everywhere, by others and the natural environment (through storms, catastrophes, etc.) because we partake in a collective reality. But when you gain a foothold into this *warring* state of mind that's frequently (*not always*) dictating distraction and disorder in the world, you'll recognize your ability to recreate a new future grounded in balance and harmony for yourself and others.

Sun Tzu bids the student to walk gently, without need to force, strive, or seek, but to allow the inner teacher to take direct action to rule the thoughts creating discord and establish a well-governed kingdom. In doing so, shifting our perception from disorder to order has its own level of *social responsibility*, giving us an unlimited opportunity to be kind and loving to others, to create a world where peace is ever-present.

When we join (our Whole mind) with others in collective harmony, we partake of the shared unity available to all living beings on a global scale.

This beautiful and effortless way of living with others is available at all times and every moment. In fact, you won't want to miss an opportunity to let a stray or careless thought pass through your mind, so as not to hurt another living being.

As a result, love blossoms, kindness reigns *effortlessly*. This is Sun Tzu's promise on the Hidden Path to Peace and Wholeness.

As we tread the path together, let us do so openly and without fear.

There is no retreat from this kind of battle.

HOW TO APPROACH THIS BOOK

The Modern Art of War is comprised of thirteen new chapters based on the original esoteric teachings and utilizes the original numbering system from the Giles translation. Each chapter contains a summary, followed by commentary that assimilates Sun Tzu's main ideas by providing ways you can apply the teachings in your own life and practice. Each chapter contains ruminations for further exploration. Some chapters include practical exercises.

To give you an idea of what's ahead, here is a chapter-by-chapter breakdown:

- **Chapter 1:** *Laying Plans*—Exploration on making a commitment to work on the disquieted mind by creating a plan of action. Addresses the most common pitfalls associated with marshaling the mind, while offering a valuable place to begin.

- **Chapter 2:** *The Costs of Waging (Mental) War*—After making a commitment in earnest, we no longer fear retreat and can begin to objectively observe what we're thinking, doing, saying, feeling, etc., to evolve into a state of Wholeness.

- **Chapter 3:** *Undertake by Stratagem*—The preliminary teaching of direct observation as a means to strategically interrupt, divide, divert, or conquer evasive thoughts to create new inroads to peace and harmony.

- **Chapter 4:** *Calculating One's Nature*—Considers the nature of thought, how it begins and creates thought-streams, skewed by the field of perception. With foreknowledge, we can regain the advantage of awareness through our Inner Sun and live more fully.

- **Chapter 5: *Rooted Concentration*—**Explores the first stage of concentration. Learn to create advantages over the usual, disordered nature or imbalances we encounter daily to effortlessly guide our focus toward unity and harmony.

- **Chapter 6: *Balancing Weak and Strong Points*—**Engage a deeper understanding of the way our mind creates duality and division so that we can strategically maintain balance and harmony on a more regular basis.

- **Chapter 7: *Calculated-Awareness Practice*—**Explores our inherent ability to *maneuver* our perception to a more disciplined and concentrated state of attention, which will provide a deeper understanding of how our thoughts multiply and stifle awareness.

- **Chapter 8: *Variations of Method*—**The discovery of the Five Advantages and the nature of thought through direct experiences: if we are aware of how thoughts arise, their strength or power to *evade* detection can be planned and responded to accordingly.

- **Chapter 9: *Contemplative-Awareness Expansion*—**The more we assert concentration and attention to clear the field of perception, the more we create equanimity as a regular state of awareness that expands... and expands!

- **Chapter 10: *Territory of the Mind*—**Now that you have an understanding of the mind in expansion, Sun Tzu offers the six most obvious ways thought appears—or rather, how we sense thought across a boundless field of perception.

- **Chapter 11: *The Nine (Impartial) Fields of Perception*—**Delve into the thirteen distinguished ways to *sense* the way thought appears. This foreknowledge will assist in maintaining a mastery of concentration and awareness to unfold peace and Wholeness.

- **Chapter 12: *The Wholehearted-Will*—**Now that you understand the field of perception, you can overcome limitations of thoughts and senses and recognize where *outbreaks* occur to restore natural balance.

- **Chapter 13:** *Discerning Frailty*—The hallmark teaching on discerning the frailty present in all things. Through frailty comes an understanding of the interconnected nature of our existence—thus, the light of the Inner Sun ushers in a state of victory!

You may benefit from first reading the entire text through once, then returning to the beginning to undertake a deeper study and incorporate what is useful into tools for daily practice. Alternatively, you might begin by reading each chapter, one at a time, then ruminating on the information and putting the applied practice to use for a designated period. Once at a comfortable level of understanding, proceed on to the next chapter. Equally, since there are a year's worth of chapters, you can engage one chapter a month, for a full year (and one month) of study.

In total, the commentary is meant to support your exploration of the lessons in *The Modern Art of War,* while you actively engage in daily life *now,* not some future, distant moment. Applying the work through a hobby, skill, or trade can be beneficial, since repetition on a single task allows the mind to engage concentration and focus more fully, over a period of time, and in steps that eventually arrive at mastery.

For example, if you are a writer, rock climber, a dancer, a singer, actor, a race-car driver, a sculptor, a knitter, an engineer, mechanic, athlete, musician, or an inventor, and so on, practicing your craft can create a means to develop Sun Tzu's observation practice, along with many of the other teachings found in this book.

Equally, our daily life provides an endless stream of tasks that allows us to engage Sun Tzu's teachings to master our mind: cleaning a toilet, cooking, playing, washing laundry, gardening, talking to customers, stocking shelves or packing boxes, sweeping, or making tea are all incredible ways to learn patience and calmness.

Every action counts. The key is to begin in the next unfolding moment. *Join me now!*

When you make the *day* your meditation, a moment-to-moment ceremony or celebration—a singular, ceaseless expression that is present— the day-to-day worries gradually recede. You will gradually give up the war of constant-thinking, which keeps you from observing who you truly are. When we settle the war within, it is in our grasp to become a Master Sun.

May you be victorious.

Ruminations: The Path to Peace and Wholeness

"Nowhere is it recorded where a student has benefited from prolonging preparation and execution of practice."

– Chapter 2

---

1. What does physical war look like to you? Draw a picture or write a poem to express it.

---

2. In contrast, what does *personal* war look like in your life? Give an example of a conflict with others you are currently embroiled in.

---

3. What examples can you give where you *knowingly* experienced your intuition?

---

4. How easy/difficult is it for you to consider that a teacher lies *within*, and that the quest for peace or wisdom also lies within, and is not external?

---

5. What do you hope to bring into your new life, now that you're embarking on Sun Tzu's Hidden Path to Peace and Wholeness?

6. What does a life of peace and harmony look like to you?

7. What skill, trade, or craft interests you, that you can utilize and apply Sun Tzu's teachings? If nothing comes to mind, what excites and inspires you? (Do this now.)

8. Share one thing you can do today that can overturn a pre-held belief about others, ushering in peace to this mini-war.

9. Consider an area of your life, or in the world, where you've observed the evidence of *what hurts one, hurts us all*. What step(s) could be taken directly to create change?

10. What do you like to do in life and how might you begin to honor it even more, and apply the teachings as you learn them?

1

LAYING PLANS

1. Sun Tzu said: the art of observing the mind is of vital importance to the Self.

2. Attaining a unified Self is a matter of life and death, a road to either safety or ruin.

3. When battling for union of the Self, there are five principles that should be taken into account in one's deliberations, in order to reach oneness with the Source.

4. They are: The Moral Law; Heaven; Earth; The General; Method and Discipline.

5–6. The Moral Law, or *Way*, causes a student to be in complete accord with their Higher Self, so they will follow it regardless, undismayed by any danger. By allowing the Higher Self to rule, the body will be in accord with the Self and not fear anything in the sea of earthly worry.

7. Heaven (Yin), or the Higher Self, must be in balance, so the student can achieve awareness, just like night balances day or cold balances heat, and the times of the seasons balance one another.

8. Earth (Yang), or the ego (or Lower Consciousness that perceives the body as a form), will undergo many obstacles, some great and small, and others that will challenge its sense of safety and make it unstable, since it will not readily give up control; thus, the student must be dedicated. Should you master the disquieted mind, you will usher in *life* for the united Self, and *death* to the ego.

9. The dedicated student (the General) on the path of Wholeness will find virtues of wisdom, sincerity, benevolence, courage, and strictness, at their command.

10. Method and Discipline are to be understood as one's ability to marshal the army of senses and desires into their rightful places, and also with maintaining one's vital energy through the *roads*,[1] into the body, which supplies one's consciousness, and controls how much vital energy is expended. (The student who endeavors to practice will be disciplined to overcome their desires and control their senses.)

11. These five senses (sight, hearing, taste, smell, and touch), should be familiar to every student: the one who knows how to control them will be victorious; the one who does not, will fail. The student who continues to give in to earthly desires derived from the senses (e.g., taste, which can lead to gluttony), will not reach Wholeness.

12. Therefore, in your deliberations, when determining the path to attain awareness, consider the following questions in order to be successful:

a. Which of the two, the Higher or the Lower Self, is imbued with the Path to Peace and Wholeness?

b. Of the two, which has more ability to succeed?

c. Which is more in balance, and therefore has the advantage, when obstacles arise? How can you bring your mind (thoughts/desires) to a state of balance?

d. On which side is Discipline most rigorously enforced?

e. Which side is more highly trained?

f. Which side shows a greater ability to remain unchanged, especially when it comes to rewards or penalties?

---

1   "Roads" or *meridians* that extend vital energy/power through the body. Sometimes referred to as chakras, from the Sanskrit, "cakra," meaning wheel, or that which turns.

13. By means of these seven considerations, the student (and teacher)[2] can forecast the mind's victory or defeat in attaining oneness with the Source.

14. The student who hearkens to the teacher's counsel (intuition) and puts it into practice will conquer the Self's delusion of form; this type of student should maintain control. But the student who doesn't follow the teacher's counsel (intuition's counsel) or put it into practice, will remain in a state of delusion and non-awareness of their whole Self; they must regain control.

15. Above and beyond intuition's/teacher's counsel, if you have knowledge of your own weaknesses, let them be known that you might also conquer them.

16. Equally, if you're not making progress with your practice, modify what you're doing accordingly.

17. All warfare of the disquieted mind—the battle to break or ascend the illusion of the earthly realm—is based on deception.[3] The Lower Self (Earth) will attempt to deceive the Higher Self (Heaven). This is a simple point, but important, as many people who start upon the path to inward peace grow restless and bored. The body, with the help of the disquieted mind, will find more exciting things to do, thus, deceiving the Self from seeking Wisdom.

18. Hence, when able to practice (e.g., observe the mind), we must seem unable, or to do so without striving. When using our *forces* (the army),[4] we must seem inactive; when our forces are near, we must make the *enemy* (conscious thoughts) believe we are far away; when far away, we must seem like we are near. To attain awareness, one needs to find stillness of the mind. The battle is in focusing the mind to a place of equanimity—a hard enough feat. The teacher (intuition) knows that the body will resist, and so, the still mind must be vigilant and steer clear of the pull of the senses.

---

2   The teacher is Intuitive-Knowing, or intuition found within. The teacher is hiding within and is not external. We only need to tune in to our intuition to *hear* the teacher.
3   When we ascribe difficulty (e.g., illness, pain, setback, trial) to any moment, we've created a division in perceiving Wholeness; thus, we can reconsider our thoughts to gain freedom from limiting points of view.
4   See Introduction, "The Army."

19. Through vigilance of the mind, the student *can* overcome the delusion of the earthly senses. Do not give in to fighting with the body/senses, for they will most certainly win. The enemy is the Self. The teacher (intuition) advises the strategy of tricking the Self into being still, thus gaining awareness.

20. If bodily senses are strong, be prepared to falter. Do what you must to avoid acknowledging the Self.

21. Do not shun your emotions, such as anger, but sit with it, so that you can understand it, conquer it, and move on. Furthermore, if you grow aggrieved or arrogant, you should avoid action and remain still.

22. As for strategies to conquer your desires and senses, be vigilant and do not allow them to gain a foothold. Separate them from other emotions, so that they are easier to unravel, understand, and overcome.

23. Additionally, use the time when you are not *risen to* (or affected by) high emotions or desires to investigate them, and move to a place where they do not control you.

24–25. It is the role of the teacher (intuition) to guide the student (conscious mind) through the levels of reaching the Self's awareness (Inner Sun). Knowing beforehand what challenges are to come will turn the weak student away. In order to reach victory or equanimity, the student should focus on the present moment and not worry about the past or what is to come.

26. Now, the student who makes many calculations before the battle is fought will win out over the disquieted mind. Likewise, the student who makes few considerations will lose. You can foresee already who will be successful and who will not be.

INTERPRETING THE LIVING WISDOM OF SUN TZU

Sun Tzu is asking the committed student on the Hidden Path to Peace and Wholeness to consider the importance of understanding the difficulty involved in attaining freedom from the disquieted mind. The reader is provided with five principles that when put into practice can assist the willing warrior to embody a deeper sense of their inherent intuition or oneness with the Inner Sun.

As we make this connection with our all-seeing awareness, we immediately begin to see changes in our day-to-day life. Though Sun Tzu warns about the immediate obstacles that we'll encounter once a commitment to the path is made. The more we plan for those obstacles, the more we can measure your success. Be vigilant and steadfast; boredom and restlessness can overcome the beginner at the onset of making changes. Anticipate the urge to push too much or be harsh and dictatorial, and take the soft approach.

In so many words, Sun Tzu is asking us to be aware of the body's needs and the mind's restlessness, and not to punish ourselves for either. We should let the sense-emotions come and go without a struggle, rather than letting them rule you.

LESSON ONE (1–4): THE QUEST FOR INNER PEACE AND WHOLENESS

On the path of self-mastery and Wholeness, Sun Tzu explains the student's commitment is a matter of life and death. In theory, once the Self is attuned to the intuition (Intuitive-Knowing), there is no longer a boundary or separation between the perceptions of dual-thinking (e.g., good/bad, hot/cold, life/death). The once selfish mind is recalibrated without the seesawing effect and can experience peace, making our decisions, choices, and purpose much easier to understand and trust.

By preparing for our journey to Wholeness, symbolized by a formal commitment, we're being asked to not waste time and to immediately establish strategies that will clear or empty the "battlefield of the mind." If we do, we can alleviate our inner suffering (e.g., fear, worry, distrust, paranoia, failure) that cloud our discernment in daily matters. As our perceptions shift, we are no longer ruled by disquieted emotions, but are given to experience inner peace.

But take notice, Sun Tzu warns that this path will lead either to safety (from cyclical existence) or to ruin (rebirth).

LESSON TWO (5–11): THE FIVE PRINCIPLES OF SELF-MASTERY

Sun Tzu's core teachings in the preliminary chapter are broken into five principles or considerations of self-mastery: *The Moral Law; Heaven; Earth; The Commander; Method and Discipline.* Each is meant to help the initiate on the Hidden Path to Peace and Wholeness to get started. Remember, this is the start of the journey (figuratively), a time when we make a personal commitment and "lay plans," so that we can be successful and realize our full potential.

Each of the five principles focuses on balance and harmony. Although war and all its components are used as symbols, we're actually clearing the battlefield of the mind, to give peace and harmony a foothold as a natural state of being. So long accustomed to noise, distraction, constant chatter, and movement, we begin to evaluate our mind, and see how it operates moment to moment. In doing so, we recognize that our "normal" state is actually stillness of mind, tranquil peace and harmony, and therefore, we can act more direct and assured in our daily affairs.

- Sun Tzu's *first principle* is the Moral Law, or the path we undertake that reestablishes our ability to *hear* that small soft voice within as the highest truth (or the Constant-Knowing). Our intuition is designed to teach the student-warrior how to relinquish fear in their daily lives—especially in the disquieted mind, which will automatically create resistance and try to "flee" by avoiding practice and training—and quiet!

  Consider the strength of the "enemy," our perpetual thoughts and perceptions, which have always been dominant and will now come under "attack," as we take up an approach to unlearn all our former behaviors, habits, and patterns. It will not surrender easily and will do much to deter the student-warrior from being diligent and steadfast. Since our inner-awareness is pure and all-knowing, and exists unimpacted by our thoughts or emotions, it can be harnessed as our natural state rather than being ruled by imbalanced and uncertain emotions constantly impacted by exterior circumstances.

  We are essentially going to take up a practice to unlearn all our former behaviors, habits, and patterns. Sun Tzu explains that we need to let go of fear to bring this unity about between Higher and Lower Consciousness, and create balance without the interference of (perceived) outside distractions. We're not trying to "destroy" our thoughts, but to allow our natural state of peace to become our ruling state of experience. In doing so, our individuality, our specialness, no longer hinged by the unpredictability of emotion, becomes more in tune and we begin to live from our inherent purpose and pure-knowing.

- The *second principle*, represented as Heaven (or Yin), explains that awareness is born out of our ability to keep our Yin nature or conscious-awareness *in balance* as we engage in daily (outward) activity. First, we need to recognize a quiet mind is our natural state and allow it space to gain a footing. In doing so, we begin to tap into our "felt-sense," that internal compass that gives us the go-ahead. If you've ever just known to do something and did it, like taking a different route to work, and later learned you avoided a delay, then you've experienced Intuitive-Knowing. Imagine having that knowledge with you all the time!

  Sun Tzu is suggesting that we can achieve this union by not giving our thoughts—like doubt and worry—the main stage to the show of our daily activity. Instead, we allow thoughts and emotions to pass, without question or hindrance, and give room for intuition to solely guide us. To get there, we need to trust and prepare a quiet mind as our natural, everyday, existence.

- The *third principle* is Earth (Yang) and represents the ego (or Lower Consciousness that perceives the body as a form), which does not want to give up control or its perception of form. Most of the resistance will be felt in the material realm, as soon as you start to practice (meaning, you're undertaking awareness to no longer be led by your thoughts and senses). The Self will not feel safe—it will feel like it is heading toward oblivion or death—but if you can persevere, Sun Tzu says, the result will be eternal life for the united Self or consciousness.

- The Commander, or *fourth principle*, represents the "one who sees" and witnesses the battle, and seeks to be the guiding force for the two minds (intuitive and ego) to reach a state of harmony that will usher in wisdom, sincerity, benevolence, courage, and strictness at their command. This will in turn usher in order and victory, or in this case, self-awareness and oneness with all creation (the Constant-Knowing).

- The *fifth principle* to consider is Method and Discipline, the tools that allow the student-warrior to bring ultimate balance, unity, and harmony with their senses, while also maintaining their vital energy (which supports conscious thought). The more the student practices, the more experienced they'll become with employing the strategies, and the more likely they'll lessen the risk of failure. Sun Tzu's approach is methodical because she anticipates how the student can fail and implements a technique to bypass failure in the hope that the student will continue on to victory.

Lastly, in *Laying Plans*, Sun Tzu reminds the student-warrior of the power of the five senses, (sight, hearing, taste, smell, and touch). If we *can't* control them, we're bound to fail. As we make a formal commitment and begin to implement the exercises Sun Tzu provides, we must recognize that the senses, which can trigger emotions, will need to be mastered to reach self-realization and awareness (or non-duality).

Mastering, here, implies understanding and softness, as opposed to suppression or hardness. Another helpful word is *surrender*, since we allow our thoughts to pass unrestricted, or we might surrender a habit, which might create a feeling of passivity or weakness, but it's very much a choice and a command, one given freely, rather than force. Essentially, we're relinquishing the hold our emotions, thoughts, and senses have on what we will do and how we will act, in favor of working with the intuition as our highest authority.

For example, if you would like to relinquish the control a particular food has on you, your senses or emotions will create a war in your mind by indicating that you're "giving up" something or going without. Take a moment to investigate *why* you believe you're giving something up in the first place. Often times, we can discover the origin of the habit and uproot its control.

Likewise, pain and illness are other experiences we cater to with negative language and a lineage of fear; we've deemed them "bad" or something to be rid of, since both are concepts constructed with negative associations. But in fact, they are ideas we ourselves decide, perceive, and create our reality from, and so they can be changed, shifted, or neutralized to free us from the way they can imprison us.

Ultimately, mastery over the "enemy" (our thoughts, senses) then prevails by asserting an unmovable will, as we shall see in more detail, that need not be aggressive or hostile, but discerning and firm.

LESSON THREE (12): CONSIDER THE HARD QUESTIONS

Sun Tzu is asking the student to consider the hard questions—even before the journey has begun—in order to lay the groundwork to further understand how hard the struggle will be. We need to first ask, which is stronger: our intuitive or conscious thinking-mind? Which one is more likely to succeed?

Depending on where you see yourself on the "path" will decide your answers. If you're just beginning to gain awareness of how the mind operates, more often, it is your material mind that is most in control, since it's caught up in the daily operations of life whenever difficulty arises. But gradually this can and will change.

Furthermore, Sun Tzu is asking, when difficulty arises and struggle abounds, how are you most likely to respond? Whether you're just beginning to cultivate present awareness or have spent years bringing the mind under control, the thinking-mind can still step in and make demands to keep you from evolving a state of Wholeness. Practice, then, isn't reserved for the meditation room, but occurs in the next unfolding moment and every situation—*it is the next decision you make* that essentially determines the answer.

We can *always* try again.

As you continue on Sun Tzu's Hidden Path to Peace and Wholeness, be attentive. Don't put off doing the work *right now*. Sun Tzu is asking you to consider *which side is responding* in *each* activity. Over time, as you change, you will gradually see improvements, and notice whether or not the intuitive mind *can* or *is* usurping control over the habitual thinking-mind (and vice versa).

Most importantly, at this preliminary stage, we're given the ability to forecast "victory" or "defeat" for ourselves, in attaining oneness with the Whole.

LESSON FOUR (13–23): ENCOUNTERING CHALLENGES

By reviewing the questions Sun Tzu provides, we can recognize our weaknesses and grow determined to make changes, to do something different, even if the journey is difficult. Sun Tzu is asking: *Are you up for the challenge?* If we put the teachings into practice, we can change the course of our lives and "conquer" the habituated thinking-mind's hold. When we know our own weaknesses, we need to address them to learn about ourselves, so we can grow. And if we're not making progress, we can then easily make modifications to what we're doing accordingly.

Equally, Sun Tzu teaches that in order to break the illusion of the earthly realm (or day-to-day environment), the student-warrior needs to be vigilant of their own ability to deceive. The only enemy you'll find on the journey is within—even when others seem to be making life difficult, you'll soon discover it's your own mind that's creating the disturbance.

When we are bothered by something external (e.g., a dog barking, noisy traffic), it may seem like the subject of our agitation, but it's actually our perception making it so. This may be a hard idea to consider because instinctively our emotions make us feel bothered when we hear noise or come into conflict with others. But if you were to investigate further, you may eventually realize it is actually *your choice*, as your emotion arising from that experience is the root of the disturbance.

As we put Sun Tzu's teachings into practice, we gain new perceptions, and gradually recognize that it's only *our* mind that is ascribing the irritation, which is *unnatural*. With practice, the more we work with disciplining the mind and desires, the more we will see who is really intruding on whom, for example, as when we blame external forces such as a bad parent, bully-boss, pain, and so on, for our (perceived) woes. The sooner we can accept responsibility for *everything* in our life and refrain from blaming others, the sooner we'll increase our awareness and be able to conquer our difficulties and make enduring changes.

Sun Tzu also warns that the disquieted mind will try to deceive the warrior, who will grow bored and tired quickly. Without vigilance, we can turn from the quest for wisdom and return to our old ways and habits. The key to "winning" the battle over thoughts is letting go of striving—our ability to work on our mind without pursuing a result or an outcome is essential to Sun Tzu's practice all day and in every activity. The goal is to not be pulled one way or the other, but to allow the mind room to experience equanimity or calm-balance no matter the occasion.

And we're not suddenly devoid of our goals or ambition, but we can evolve from acting out of fear or worry, to become more detached from the outcome, allowing the future to form *naturally* and in accord with our peaceful intentions.

To this end, Sun Tzu asks the student-warrior to approach each moment with vigilance, especially when the body/senses begin to fight for attention (for example, when you feel tired, lazy, anxious, etc.). She warns, "Do what you must to avoid acknowledging the Self." Moreover, we need not suppress our emotions, but simply not allow them a footing—let them come and go like clouds or cars passing ours on the highway. If we're angry, we should acknowledge it; there's no need to feel degraded, but rather view it as part of our imperfect-perfection and carry on.

Gradually, we will see these responses as habituated actions, which no longer serve us, and we will effortlessly let go, ushering in our core harmony. If you happen to experience a moment "risen to high emotion," then investigate your emotional state and work with it—understand it—until it's no longer controlling you.

LESSON FIVE (24–26): FINDING YOUR INNER TEACHER

The teacher's role is to guide the student-warrior and to anticipate what challenges will arise. In this case, our intuition (Intuitive-Knowing) serves as the sole authority, the inner teacher "hiding" in plain sight that we can make a pledge to and trust wholeheartedly.

The misinterpreted phrase, *When the student is ready, a teacher will appear*, has misled students for generations into a lifelong, *external* search for a special *external* teacher, when it has only ever implied the awareness of the teacher *within*—hidden, but no less actively advocating on their behalf. *When you are ready, your hidden teacher—your intuition—will appear.*

This is why Sun Tzu is asking us to take an active role in our own *Hidden Path to Peace and Wholeness* and not to be fooled by distractions. We're asked to prepare, to lay the plans, to grow aware of the challenges we face right from the start, so that we don't turn away.

Ultimately, our goal is to be present, to work from an understanding that doesn't worry about the future or the past. By doing so, we can assess (or calculate) our own ability to foresee our success in evolving to a regular state of self-awareness. We are always working toward freeing the inner teacher—our intuition or Intuitive-Knowing—to be our guide without interference.

RECOGNIZING YOUR TRUE NATURE

On our journey to recognize our true nature, it's not enough to just *read* Sun Tzu. We need to *apply* the teachings to our daily lives and experience a constant state of present-awareness (Constant-Knowing), *which is* our natural path. If not, our thoughts or perceptions will continue to dwell in a state of war.

To begin, we can cultivate "direct observation" of our thoughts, in order to bring harmony and peace to our day-to-day moments and life. When this happens, even when we make a small effort, our outer world will react and respond to the care we're giving it. Gentleness prevails and kindness reigns, as we bring love and perfection to all we do. With time, you'll not want to let a momentary careless thought go unaccounted for in case it could go out and create a "war" or imbalance in the world.

How can we begin to apply the teachings to a daily practice?

Chapter 1 provides the preparatory step needed to recognize our mind's weaknesses. As an experienced teacher, Sun Tzu is aware of many things that will prevent our first steps on the Hidden Path to Peace and Wholeness, while also recognizing the limitations of what a student can know at this early stage.

In short, if at the beginning of your commitment, you know something that will hinder you, reveal it so that you can overcome it. Confront it, bring it out into the open, and be curious. Sun Tzu's message of preparation echoes the wisdom of the Buji proverb: "Before you climb a tree you must start at the bottom." When we lay plans, beginning "at the bottom" we have our whole journey ahead, and the knowledge of every step we will take upon it.

EXERCISE:
REFLECT ON YOUR KNOWN OBSTACLES

On your tablet or piece of paper, draw two columns. Now make a list of any obstacles and hindrances you know of. Put these in one column and in the next write a suggested solution. For example, if you were trying to establish a schedule for walking, but seem to have many things in your daily life that prevent you from undertaking a regular practice, your list might look like this example in Figure 1.

Hindrances	Solutions
Time restrictions.	Get up a half-hour earlier, or stay up a half-hour later to make time for walking.
Too tired most days.	Change my diet to include lighter, more energy-boosting foods that will give me more stamina; establish a mindset that overrules tiredness.
Can't find a good place to walk.	Research nearby parks or trails to walk in. Be open to new possibilities and aim for easily accessible places. Look into an indoor mall or power-walk the supermarket aisles.
I'm successful for three days and then something gets in the way.	Make a new commitment that honors my strong will to succeed and don't give up. If something gets in the way, inquire why I'm letting it do so. If walking is important to me, I must *willfully* find a way to succeed.

Figure 1: Example of Laying Plans

When we identify with and highlight our (perceived) limitations, we are essentially accepting responsibility for them, not trying to hide or push them away. We accept who we are at the moment, yet we're also acknowledging that we're willing to confront what might hold us back, our habits and patterns that we've been ruled by for so long. So, if you know you have something preventing you from succeeding, according to Sun Tzu, you can make adjustments to prevent failure.

When we look at the nature of what we deem an obstacle, we're also addressing our own dual-thinking. In theory, there are no obstacles, only our perception that they exist. For example, if you feel you want to lose weight and then can't stick to a diet, it creates an obstacle or sense of failure and you feel "bad." The place to start is with the "you" who believes that your current weight is a thing to reduce. Why? If you have a sense of imbalance (for example, you feel you are too heavy), you can bring the body *into balance* by making another choice in the next instant without resistance or the potential harm of labeling yourself as "bad" for having put on weight (or overeaten), or creating the duality that a better you, who weighs less, exists elsewhere (usually the future).

If we can get off the mental seesaw of here/there, heavy/not heavy, we remove the dualistic nature of how we perceive reality/our life; we free ourselves and can eat when and what we want to eat, and walk if and when we want to walk, all with harmony, not duality. It's your path—you're the General and in charge of your journey. So, take it a thought at a time with equanimity! At the same time, once you make up your mind, don't give in—if you do, then the body/senses are in control, not your mind.

Now you try. Fill in the chart (Figure 2) with a list of the (perceived) hindrances that are keeping or have kept you from beginning work on the Hidden Path to Peace and Wholeness. What things currently prevent you from creating a new balance in your life? What things have deterred you in the past? Write them down now and consider possible solutions. How can you work with those perceived hurdles to create harmony in your life by resolving those obstacles? Then, pick one and start there.

Remember that *practice* doesn't necessarily mean a specific time set aside for an activity, like meditation, prayer, or exercise—it certainly can be, and immensely helpful. But it can also suggest any pursuit throughout the day that provides the space to work with your mind and emotions. Every day, you engage difficulty and make decisions that pull you into emotional states that aren't in balance. You probably don't need to go far to find these battles.

To begin, you could make a list of hindrances you encounter throughout a typical day. An example might be when you feel your workplace is detrimental to maintaining a balanced mind—one that is not in a constant state of good/bad, happy/sad, etc., but whole or experiencing balance. What obstacles present themselves in your workplace and what can you do to create more balance on a regular basis?

Hindrances	Solutions

Figure 2: Identifying Obstacles

Preparation is key—as are organization and discipline—to cultivating a lasting practice that will establish a naturally quiet mind of self-mastery. Whether we're taking our first step or our millionth, we have much to gain by addressing what might hinder us. The more we dedicate ourselves to our new path, the more courage and discipline will be at our command.

Eventually, the more we practice, the more our "enemies" will reveal themselves and we are able to combat them. As Sun Tzu explains, knowing the obstacles ahead of time, we can lay plans to achieve success. In doing so, we're being a wise General on the battlefield of life.

THE FIRST STEP ON THE HIDDEN PATH TO PEACE AND WHOLENESS

1. Apply the teachings in Laying Plans in whatever way best reveals itself to you without fear or hindrances.

2. Craft a plan toward a new life goal or daily practice, or simply establish a plan for mastering the mind as the priority in your life.

3. Name your (perceived) weaknesses and call out any habits that will create potential obstacles. Then work to clear them, so you can achieve success.

Laying Plans is the first step on the Hidden Path to Peace and Wholeness. When we trust our ability to create change, we can make an earnest commitment toward a goal, and establish an unwavering mindset to achieve it.

Ruminations: Laying Plans

"The student who makes many calculations before the battle is fought will win out over the disquieted mind."

– Chapter 1

----

1. What is Sun Tzu saying specifically to you? Remember, it is your Hidden Path to Peace and Wholeness, and need to begin trusting your inner teacher, then apply it. What might this inner wisdom reveal to you about where you are on your personal life journey?

----

2. Of the five senses (sight, hearing, taste, smell, and touch), which one causes you the most distraction at this time? And why?

----

3. What fears in your mind keep you from pursuing an inner journey toward self-mastery?

----

4. Looking closer at Sun Tzu's questions (12) for laying plans, answer the following:

    • Which of the two Selves, Higher or Lower, is imbued with present-awareness? Of the two, which has more ability of succeeding?

    • Which is more in balance, and therefore has the advantage, when obstacles arise? How can you bring your mind (thoughts/desires) to a state of balance?

    • On which side is Discipline most rigorously enforced? Which side is more highly trained?

- Which side shows a greater ability to be unchanged when it comes to rewards or penalties?

- -

5. Can you forecast victory or defeat? What does this reveal about your own nature? Does it deter or encourage you? *Are you up for the challenges ahead?* Why or why not?

- -

6. In what ways have you *deceived* yourself and deterred your own journey on the balanced path? Give examples of where you've blamed someone else for your problems. How can you begin to take responsibility for a long-standing problem in your life? (Consider the example about the dog barking.)

- -

7. What other *calculations* can you make before preparing your mind for daily practice?

- -

8. In what way are you vigilant in guarding your mind from restless thoughts and desires throughout the day?

- -

9. Give an example when you were *not* "risen to high emotion or desire" and were able to investigate your experience in order to move toward a place where your emotions didn't control you the next time.

10. What is your greatest (perceived) weakness and how can you become knowledgeable about it, so you can "conquer" or move through it?

---

11. What activities can you incorporate into your daily Path to Peace and Wholeness—things that emphasize doing something new and different— to gain greater self-awareness of your habitual patterns?

---

12. What one small change can you make today toward your own self-wholeness and new future?

CHAPTER 2

THE COSTS OF WAGING (MENTAL) WAR

1. Sun Tzu said: the cost of waging a mental battle against the disquieted mind is equal to giving up one-thousand pieces of gold; the student should be willing to give up this cost of earthly endeavors to advance their efforts. In physical war, you would organize one thousand swift chariots and one thousand armored soldiers, along with all the provisions to support the army both at home and in the field; in a war happening in the disquieted mind, these things are equal to our thoughts, desires, habits, and distractions—a burden (or cost) that keeps us from succeeding.

2. When the student sits to practice, if victory (or success) in calming the mind (emotions/thoughts/desires) is long in coming, then their senses will grow dull and their enthusiasm will be dampened. If you try to undertake too much at one time, you will exhaust your strength.

3. The more you postpone taking action, the more your resources—including your vital energy—will be strained and cause an imbalance that will hinder success.

4. When you find yourself in the state where you have exhausted your strength and resources, and your enthusiasm is low and mind dull, situations (desires/thoughts/people/events) will arise to take advantage of you. If this happens, even the wise will find it hard to avert the consequences that will ensue.

5. Thus, those who are hasty in preparing to execute action (to gain control of the mind) will experience long delays, but those who exercise cleverness and preparation will not.

6. There is no record of a student ever having benefited from prolonging preparation to execute practice.

7. Only someone who is well acquainted with the nature of the mind, and all its obstacles, can thoroughly understand the most beneficial way of proceeding.

8. The skillful practitioner does not need to make a second commitment, having made the first in earnest, nor will they need to resupply their passion, having taken precautions to maintain it.

9. By maintaining your vital energy and vigor for the practice, you will begin to feed on the "enemy"—that is, you will begin to conquer or calm your thoughts/desires/habits that are costly to your natural state of equanimity; in doing so, you will have need of less and thus have fewer wants, allowing you to endure and succeed.

10. If you have a disquieted mind, which means that you are weakened by the constant nagging of wants and desires, it will feel like you're always working at a distance and never gaining any ground. In the same way that fighting a physical war from afar will drain funding, engaging the same unhealthy patterns and habits will physically and mentally drain you.

11. On the other hand, if you are close to recognizing your weaknesses when working with your unquiet mind, and you act to counter them, then you will build up strength and vigor that won't easily be drained away.

12. When your vital energy is drained away, the senses will dull and demand more.

13–14. If this loss of vital energy continues, then it will not only strengthen the "enemy" (restless thoughts and desires) but strip the body of health and stamina. It is like an exhausted army going into battle: it will face continued exhaustion, wounds, further draining of resources, and even death.

15. Hence a wise student (or General) makes it a point to quiet the mind's restless thoughts and desires. Quieting one thought is equal to an army gaining a cartload of provisions; it will nourish and strengthen both mind and body, not weaken them.

16. Now in order to continue this "attack" and regain control of the mind, the student needs to be encouraged to see the benefits of defeating unnecessary thoughts/desires and the rewards that follow.

17. Therefore, when a detrimental thought/desire/habit is replaced with a beneficial one, a rewarding shift in perception occurs. Replacing old thoughts/habits and patterns with new ones is done in a gentle way, like the soldier captured in war who is treated fairly.

18. This is called using conquered thoughts to increase one's strength.

19. In a war of the mind then, let your great objective be the aim of victory, not procrastination.

20. Thus, it may be understood that you have chosen the course of your own fate: peace or peril of the mind.

INTERPRETING THE LIVING WISDOM OF SUN TZU

As we continue on the Hidden Path to Peace and Wholeness, Sun Tzu is asking us to consider the costs of engaging in action to gain control over the restless, disquieted mind. The type of *action* we need to consider will prepare us to do "battle" for Wholeness.[1] We must plan and prepare in the same way as if we were planning to go to war: we wouldn't simply feed the army, but would also need to maintain the chariots and advisors, as well as care for those supporting us at home. If even one small detail is missed, the whole operation suffers.

Failure is one of the greatest deterrents in the long war to achieve the victory of a balanced mind. If we're not vigilant against the thought-disturbances that can harm our concentration—or if we don't guard our responses that are often habituated—then when we undergo a "battle" of difficulty or personal conflict, early on, we may not have the energy or will to endure for long. As a result, we can end up both mentally and physically tired and give up, accepting failure.

Even if we have those feelings, we don't need to commit a second time—Sun Tzu assures us that there is no need to start over, but we can resume where we are, abandon the feeling of defeat, and begin anew. In doing so, we won't feel we've lost the war, but simply *one* battle. And because we made our commitment in earnest, we can continue on with confidence.

At the same time, we can consider the benefits of asserting control over the disquieted mind. Control, in this instance, means awareness of what we are thinking. We can choose not to be carried away by an unruly mind any longer and instead win the "war" by viewing our thoughts objectively.

If, for example, we are used to experiencing our disquieted mind, we may trust it over any other experience, or believe if we have *no thought*, we'll be devoid of emotion or lose our identity. On the contrary, we *gain* freedom by allowing room for a deeper discernment or intuition to arise. This connection is deeper and all-knowing, and becomes the internal compass we trust.

Further, Sun Tzu tells us our efforts need only be small to have big results. One *old* thought or habit replaced with a *new* one, in a gentle way—meaning not forced or done through harshness—will bring about a notable shift in our consciousness that will continue to offer rewards. If we can become

---

1   Be mindful that this is figuratively stated, as we exist in present awareness, but are perceiving it as obstructed.

masters over our own thoughts and habits, and develop change through calmness, we can create a foundation for our success.

EXERCISE: PREPARE YOUR MIND

Sun Tzu is asking us to prepare our body and mind for the gradual changes that are on the way, both physically, and to our perception, which with consistent effort will lead to victory (union with our Inner Sun). You may wish to write down your responses to help you get them clear in your mind. To fully undertake this adventure, ask yourself:

- Are you taking care of your body in a way that will support it long-term?

- Are you letting go of things in your life that no longer serve you materially or emotionally?

- Are you continuing the cycle of stress, worry, and fatigue, to meet demands, continuously defeating your chances at self-mastery?

- Are you considering self-care of the mind for the "long war"? What does that look like for you?

- How are your thoughts acting and advocating for the same patterns and mindsets, creating the illusion of your limitation?

By knowing the answers ahead of time, you can prepare yourself for various obstacles on the journey ahead. You will experience a range of emotions and reactions, from a sense of progress and joy to frustration, defeat, and exhaustion. Being aware of what to expect will boost your determination to persevere.

LESSON ONE (1): COMMITTING TO THE HIDDEN PATH TO PEACE AND WHOLENESS

When we make a commitment to self-mastery, Sun Tzu explains we must be willing to give up our "gold" to proceed. In other words, it needs to have value for us. In so many words, what are you willing to give up to fully commit to your personal freedom from a disquieted mind? Are you willing to put all your faith into your new potential future, or are you only willing to commit halfway? You have to be *all* in, or you will very easily return to what you know habitually and are comfortable with.

If you *are* willing to give up all your gold—that is, to make an earnest commitment, then you won't need "resupplying" along the way. Start with a half-hearted ambition—or only give up *some of the gold*—and you're bound to falter and not gain victory because you know retreat is still an available option. You then take the easier route, returning "home," or stay in your usual circumstances, unchanged.

It goes without saying that the gold is also symbolic for giving up the belief in the value of the material world. As we make a full commitment, we give up or shift our perception of the outer world (the "gold" that is only an illusion), and surrender the way we've always done things. We let go of our perceived way of thinking, which brings us a new freedom to create (and act) on something new. It is fueled by the will, which is fully energized when unimpeded by distraction of thought, and then has a clear channel to act in partnership with the intuition and accomplish anything, and never tire.

Ultimately, when we give up the illusion of the material world (symbolized by the gold), we gain entry to the inward "gold" of Wholeness that is eternal.

LESSON TWO (2–3): THE ART OF EFFORTLESS-ALLOWING

At the onset of beginning any change, especially one that requires consistency in practice, Sun Tzu warns us that our enthusiasm for it can easily start to wane. As a result, we might begin to push, strive, or force things along, but this will only tire the student, and deplete the body of vital energy (the will) making it difficult to continue.

Remember, this is a gentle war, one that requires the student to go inward to win greater understanding of the way the mind works. It's a battle that doesn't need any *doing*, but the opposite of what we've been taught: *effortless-allowing*. If the student-warrior *pushes* to do more, *expects* more, *strives* more, then they will become weakened or discouraged, and open to the temptation of outside influences from daily life, people, and events, which can take advantage of a weakened will, making it harder to stay on course.

We have all experienced moments when we begin something new, and we are full of vigor and enthusiasm to succeed. Gradually, the longer we do it, we can easily get bored or lose steam, or we may not see results fast enough; we can face external obstacles or encounter people around us who might stir up our doubt and deter our progress. Rather than make progress, we can end up in a type of battle between our new life and the old one we're trying to give up.

The more we (figuratively) fight for ground, the more prone we are to experience fatigue and loss of energy and determination, especially as our brain is literally hardwired to repeat the program, making the "battle" to write a new one seem impossible. Meanwhile, the outside world—our daily life—carries on around us, drawing us back to the familiar and putting us at risk of giving up.

Sun Tzu explains that even a well-trained warrior will have a hard time getting back to their practice once fatigued and feeling they are a failure. In truth, when we work harder to get somewhere, we are acting from the illusion that there is a future place where we will be perfect and no longer struggling; that place only exists in the present moment, unhindered by restless thoughts. The contradiction we face in Sun Tzu's practice is that through experiencing a quiet mind, we essentially stop waging war within ourselves.

A peaceful mind is possible when we bring the soldiers of the senses under our command. But if we charge in shouting orders at ourselves to act and do, we miss the progression, the growth that comes through a shifting perception that sees the reality of the given situation for what it is: one that is neither *this* nor *that* but *is*—a state of present awareness that is constantly evolving, and can be experienced, not hurried.

Through stillness, *we become*.

LESSON THREE (5–7): PLANNING AHEAD AND EXECUTING

To prevent failure, Sun Tzu advises the student to be aware *ahead of time* what can happen if problems arise. But we can't only plan, we have to get to work, and in doing so, we will inevitably begin to face obstacles. Knowing your weaknesses and what obstacles can arise from those weaknesses, you can strategize to avoid or divert failure, ensuring potential success.

For example, say you have an addiction to chocolate and would like to regain control over it. You might plan to keep it out of your house, knowing that if you see it, you'll probably eat it. Planning ahead in this way, you're more likely to succeed. Equally, if you know a holiday is right around the corner and someone special might surprise you with a box of your favorite sweet stuff, you can plan ahead and take action by explaining you no longer eat it, and can avoid failure.

Sun Tzu is imparting the wisdom to be honest with our initial preparation. If our thoughts are bound up in the past, we may find it difficult to trust a new idea or way forward that can create change. Equally, we're at risk of procrastination if we take too long to prepare, plan, and execute. Consider this as you put your intentions into motion.

We might set a goal, prepare for weeks, even imagine ourselves engaging our intention—and when the time comes to get to work, we put it off until the next day. A week can go by with excuses and before we know it, we are waylaid in failure and inertia, having never started in the first place.

Knowing how our thoughts work to create obstacles to our success, we can recognize that we have the potential for procrastination ahead of time. Be aware of it and take action to win victory rather than retreat to the usual habit. We have to be fully *in*. Commit, plan, and execute.

Once we've committed in earnest, we try, and if we fail, we don't give up or retreat; we keep going. If we do this, we will see results.

LESSON FOUR (8–9): THE IMPORTANCE OF OBSTACLES

Because obstacles are a natural part of taming the mind, when we come up against them, it will feel like we're being challenged and we're failing. But we're not. It's part of evolving and learning about the nature of the disquieted mind.

Failure is a constructed illusion: as one obstacle arises to challenge our resolve, we can feel lost, especially when things don't go as planned. As we center our goals with a calm mind, we will gradually see all our efforts are the *same effort*, and our commitment as *one long commitment*.

Using the example of breaking your addiction to chocolate, you might go a month without eating chocolate, and then find yourself at an office party and decide to treat yourself to a chocolate dessert. The next morning, you might wake up feeling like you've lost your way and failed yourself. But it's just another perception of the mind, one that you can relearn by simply choosing again.

Over time, your perception will shift again, and whether you eat chocolate or not is irrelevant—you simply do or don't, and are not attached to it either way. The moment the desire and emotion connected to chocolate no longer controls you, that's victory.

In the process of overcoming obstacles, each time we tumble back to the beginning, we don't need to make a *second* commitment, not if we've already made the first in earnest. If you set out toward your goal with sincerity, then even when it feels like you've failed, you can keep going— the understanding that comes with the obstacle is what is actually taking you forward. It may not feel like it, but if we're sincere, then our willfulness won't wane but allow us to pick up and go on courageously.

In actuality, the difficulty is the path—the obstacle—that allows us an opportunity to act in partnership with our intuition, to peel back our perceptions and grow. Each battle allows us a foothold to conquer or calm our thoughts/desires/habits. Once we overcome the obstacle, we return to power and move on in our journey. Over time, we notice changes in the way we go about our lives, no longer swayed by emotions or careless thoughts, but directed by the Generalship of a unified mind.

In time, as we marshal our thoughts and learn the way they imprison us, we will need less and have fewer wants, which will help us deepen our practice. When a student comes to a wall in the (metaphorical) forest, they may turn around, but the Master will keep walking until they discover the way around it. Our goal is to not be deterred, but to work with our thoughts to free ourselves from their perceived control.

LESSON FIVE (10–17): A STRONG-MINDED PRACTICE

Like an exhausted army going into battle, if we're unable to focus and are weakened by the constancy of wants/desires, we'll face continued exhaustion, wounds, further drains on our resources (coffers and supplies), and even death. When we allow our desires/wants to win our attention, we may even develop or strengthen unhealthy patterns and habits, which in turn may physically and mentally drain us and stunt our momentum.

Our goal is to be the wise warrior and work diligently on quieting the restless mind filled with emotions and desires that will pull us from equilibrium and balance. If we're feeling anger, we need to be open and explore that anger, to work with it to find and return to balance, as opposed to lashing out and giving up. As Sun Tzu puts it, "Quieting one thought is equal to an army gaining a cartload of provisions; it will nourish and strengthen both mind and body, not weaken it."

We need to encourage our efforts and see the benefits that come from developing a practice that fortifies a strong will. In doing so, we're more apt to reinforce our positive traits, leading to a healthier body and mind. We also won't be so easily drained and will have the energy and willpower to continue on. Seeing these rewards, we'll be more encouraged to continue.

At the same time, if we can actually replace the old, negative habits (our usual way of thinking) with new, beneficial thoughts, we'll experience a "rewarding shift in perception." We do this gently, "like the soldier captured in war who is treated fairly."

LESSON SIX (18–20): CHOOSING YOUR FUTURE

Sun Tzu's method is to use our conquered thoughts to increase our strength to win victory over the mind and its usual habits. When doing so, we let go of procrastination, shirk off tiredness, confusion, disappointment, and the like, and claim our own fate as we progress toward "peace of the mind" and self-awareness.

In theory, if you were to free your mind of even *half* of its zillions of thoughts generated a day, you would likewise free up the energy it takes to maintain them. The energy no longer used on old thoughts in turn can be used toward a worthy goal. Sun Tzu explains: you get to choose the course of your future in every instant and thought—will it be peace or peril? As each thought unfolds into the next moment, you can willfully exert a new choice and win victory.

More often, without realizing it, we're continually choosing our future and our fate. Most will blame circumstances, people, governments—anyone but themselves—for their lot in life. But you actually get to decide what happens in the next moment, even if you've tried and failed a thousand times before, with your next new decisions, the future can be different.

Be encouraged to follow the steps Sun Tzu provides to win peace for yourself.

REFUSE TO RETREAT

Each time you actively choose to be more aware of your thoughts, you are affirming your commitment to self-mastery. Begin now by establishing a daily observation practice through an activity (for example, when walking, sitting, running, meditating, or cooking), and commit to it for one day, then one week, then one month, then three months, then one year.

Hold nothing back.

Plan, but don't procrastinate.

Each day, find time to review what is working and what's not. Ask yourself, which thoughts keep you from a quiet mind? Rather than forcing or ridding yourself of those thoughts, how can you be curious about them—enough to discover something deeper that needs to change internally?

When you begin to make changes in your life, you also start to see any obstacles that might arise to keep you from your personal, life-affirming victories. As you bring awareness to your thinking process, you will begin to experience a deep serenity that essentially carries you into the next moment, creating a new future.

We decide the future; we decide our commitment; we decide if we will give up when we face obstacles. But here's the thing—the more we can plan, prepare, act, and encourage ourselves, the more we will make gradual changes—and these small steps *will* lead to victory!

RENEWING YOUR COMMITMENT

It's very easy to feel excited and energized when we first undertake the practice of mastering the mind. But as soon as we face a problem or an obstacle—it can seem like someone or something attempts to deter us—we can get easily discouraged. But we are responsible for our choices. This is when you need to regroup and try again. Always be willing to take one more step toward the goals or dreams you want to fulfill in life.

To get started, you can review the commitment you've made on the Hidden Path to Peace and Wholeness. Ask yourself the following questions to begin exploring your possible day-to-day setbacks. Writing down your answers in a journal may help you to get a clearer picture.

- Are there areas in your life holding you back from achieving your goals? Name them and begin planning ways to overcome your perceived setbacks.

- What steps can you make to give up the "gold" and commit fully?

- What small efforts can you make to ensure that you are taking care of your body and vital energy, so that you can endure the rigors you might face on this path? Check in intuitively to see what's needed and act accordingly.

- Could you eat in a way that is more natural or in balance with yourself intuitively, or could you introduce exercise or an energy-building activity, like walking, painting, or gardening? What physical hindrances arise? What mental obstacles arise? How can you shirk off your habituated way of thinking and start anew?

- Do you do enough reflecting and reviewing to see where you can make ongoing improvements? Begin a journal. At the end of each day, review what battles you've fought, where wisdom won out over difficulty, and how you made changes. This introspection will allow you to plan, accordingly, how to increase success the next day.

No matter what challenges arise, see it as an opportunity and try once more. So long as you try again, you can never be defeated.

THE SECOND STEP ON THE HIDDEN PATH TO PEACE AND WHOLENESS

1. Apply the teachings in the Cost of Waging (Mental) War in whatever way best reveals itself to you without holding anything back.

2. Consider those things that would waste your energy, distract you, make you give up, and craft a plan to say "yes" to what serves your path and inward success.

3. Review your efforts each day and be aware of anything (for example, your perceptions of outer circumstances, acquaintances) that pulled you away from your seat of power over the mind.

The Costs of Waging (Mental) War is the second step on the Hidden Path to Peace and Wholeness. When we know what will drain our vital energy and cause us loss and suffering, we can make an earnest effort to avoid it, saying "no" to distractions and people/circumstances that don't benefit our goals and life purpose. If we do, we'll have great strength to go the distance to establish an unwavering mind that's invincible.

Ruminations: Costs of Waging (Mental) War

"Those who are hasty in preparing to execute action (in gaining control of the mind) will experience long delays, but those who exercise cleverness and preparation will not."

– Chapter 2

---

1. Sun Tzu warns us not to take on too much all at once. How can you lessen your day-to-day "burden," in order to apply the teachings in steps?

---

2. In what ways do you prolong preparation of a goal and procrastinate? How can you begin to make progress on your Hidden Path to Peace and Wholeness?

---

3. Give an example of where you tried to undertake too much at one time, exhausting your strength. Using Sun Tzu's advice, what might you do differently next time?

---

4. Describe a time when you felt exhausted, to the point of abandoning your goal, or a time when your strength and resources—your enthusiasm—was so low that you felt you couldn't go on. Using Sun Tzu's advice, what can you do to avoid this in the future?

---

5. Sun Tzu is asking us to choose peace or peril of the mind. How have you broken commitments that were important to you?

---

6. Sun Tzu tells us we *don't need to make a second commitment, having made the first in earnest.* What can you do to move forward, to let go of the feeling of failure and to gently continue on in earnest?

---

7. Our efforts need only be small to have big results. What one small thing can you do that will benefit your success today?

---

8. What does self-care look like to you? How can you carve out special time each day to support your need for meditation/quiet?

---

9. Sun Tzu tells us that one *old* thought or habit replaced with a *new* one is a step forward toward self-mastery. What single, old thought can you replace with a new one and what might be the change going forward to create a new you?

---

10. What thoughts weaken you with a constant nagging of wants/desires, keeping you from victory?

----

11. If you could change one idea about yourself to step into a new future, what would it be?

----

12. Describe a time when you attempted to make changes in your life and *succeeded*. Being honest, what do you know about yourself today that you can use in your plan for victory?

3

UNDERTAKE BY STRATAGEM

1. Sun Tzu said: it is best to take back the territory of the mind whole, rather than to allow ignorance to shatter one's attention. Equally, the goal is to gain full control of thoughts, as opposed to allowing them to linger, splinter, or multiply, making them more difficult to quell and overcome.

2. Hence, it is advised to confront your mind's resistance when working with thoughts; do so in a way that does not insinuate fault, but rather approach them with inquiry.

3. Thus, the highest form of discipline is to not give into the pull of your thoughts; the next best thing is to stop them at the intersection into another thought; the next action is to stop a thought at the root; the worst action is to grow angry when you cannot control them.

4. The rule is to not grow angry with your lack of mental control whenever possible. The preparation of the mind can take up to three months; along with another three months before you are able to silence one thought.

5. The student who is irritated and impatient with their inability to control the mind will attack their thoughts with anger, which will give rise to a swarm of more thoughts and irritations. As a result, your enthusiasm and ambition will lose momentum, while your mind continues to be restless. Such are the disastrous effects of engaging anger and impatience.

6. Therefore, the skilled student will subdue their thoughts without resistance; the student takes over and overcomes their thoughts without anger or frustration, thus, not prolonging advancement.

7. With their mind in a state of concentration, the student will continue to assert their mastery over the whole of their being, and thus, without losing themself, they will eventually triumph. This is the method of tackling the mind by stratagem.

8. It is the rule, when battling our mind, if our thoughts are busy, we can surround them, divide them, then gradually gain control over them.

9. In the case when our thoughts are equally matched—meaning that they are working hard to distract us and will not allow us to reach a state of concentration—then we can remain and work on regaining control; if our thoughts have an advantage over us, then we are best to avoid them for the time being; if our thoughts have a really big advantage over us, we should not engage but try again at another time.

10. Hence, if you are obstinate and try to regain control over thoughts that have great strength over you, you will not succeed but be overwhelmed.

11. Now the student is the guardian of the mind; if they have control and concentration, their intuition (Intuitive-Knowing) will grow and be strong; but if they have shortcomings, their concentration will weaken the connection.

12. There are three ways the student can bring misfortune to their path/ practice:

13. (1) By trying to *command* or force the disquieted mind to act a certain way, ignorant that it cannot yield by force.

14. (2) By attempting to *govern* the disquieted mind in the same way as they do their material life, ignorant that strength comes in *not-doing*, rather than action.

15. (3) By initiating actions *without discernment*, ignorant that the disquieted mind can adapt to new circumstances, which will further weaken the confidence of the student.

16. But when the mind's thoughts are out of control, it can stir up the senses, causing the whole being to be in a state of disorder, making victory short in coming.

17. Thus, we may know that there are Five Essentials for Victory over the disquieted mind:

a. The student will win who knows when to take action and when to resist.

b. The student will win who knows how to handle both the superior and inferior thoughts and distractions.

c. The student will win whose mind and senses are aligned in a unified goal.

d. The student will win, who prepared themself, waits to engage their thoughts, and allows them no power.

e. The student will win who has a healthy body,[1] one that can sustain the amount of practice needed, and will not interfere in one's advancement.

Victory over the disquieted mind lies in the knowledge of these five points.

18. Hence the saying: *If you know yourself and the nature of your mind (and what you're up against), then you need not fear the result of a hundred encounters. If you know yourself and not the nature of your mind, for every victory gained you will also suffer defeat. If you know neither yourself nor the nature of your mind, you will fail every time you practice.*

---

1   The inference to a healthy body includes regulating the flow of vital energy toward the "one eye," an alignment that brings about Whole-Awareness. Equally, it suggests maintaining the physical body's health for longevity to ensure the duration of time necessarily to complete it.

INTERPRETING THE LIVING WISDOM OF SUN TZU

Sun Tzu is urging the student to undertake a conscious strategy to become their own Master Sun. In order to win victory, we need to trust the teacher (intuition). We aren't given complicated instructions, nor are we led astray by the promise of a special training sure to change our life. Instead, we're given very simple, timeless knowledge and asked to apply it.

More importantly, as we develop a new awareness, it can become a natural way of life that acts as an exchange between our perceptions (for example, dual-thinking and emotions), to experience Wholeness (the Constant-Knowing), available to us at all times.

If we're willing, Sun Tzu shows us the way to regain self-mastery over the *whole* mind, not just a piece of it. It's easy to fool ourselves, once we've made a small change, to believe we're done. But this is a *continual* battle and will take constant vigilance over our thoughts: it is a way of life without an end, a cycle that will repeat.

As the "armies" of concentration are sent to wage war against the restless thoughts, we can learn to cut them off at the onset, and prevent them from multiplying. In doing so, we're essentially surrounding the thought, keeping it from advancing (or creating more of the emotion behind it) and thus, can gain an advantage of peace or calm that will carry us forward to victory.

But Sun Tzu cautions that when we begin to marshal our disquieted mind, we'll be prone to frustration and anger; we'll believe the thoughts (or enemy army) greater, and in our effort to stop the thoughts, must not restrict or use force. We may begin to complicate it or go elsewhere, feeling uncomfortable. The more we struggle, the more we'll witness our own weakness, and grow more obstinate; thus, failure will come easily.

This is the school for the mind, where it takes practice to learn a skill. When you master your mind and bring your thoughts into an unmoving state of concentration, you experience your pure Self and "know" who you *are*—period. Not who you *were* or who you *will be*, which creates limitation, but who you are *now*. Infinitely and without boundary.

LESSON ONE (1–6): MASTERING YOUR THOUGHTS
According to Sun Tzu, our battle is for the *full* territory, not a piece of it, or in this case, *our whole mind.* Just like on the battlefield, if you attack an army and cannot take it whole, it can splinter off and regroup. In the battlefield of the disquieted mind, we're asked to use the weapon of concentration to quell the *full* thought. If not, it will keep multiplying and be difficult to overcome.

We must be proactive to confront what our mind is engaging, and question it not with blame but investigation. For example, if you are a runner and you go for an afternoon run and strain your hamstring muscle, your mind will immediately pull you into a thought-battle over what comes next. You will essentially leave your seat of power over both the body and mind. First, the body will focus on the sensation of pain and win your attention, and second, your mind will begin to multiply thoughts about what to do. If you allow the thoughts to roam freely, like a wayward army, they will infiltrate the mind incessantly.

Sun Tzu is asking you to actively quell the thoughts before this unabating war happens. Otherwise, it will become too much to overcome. One thought becomes 10,000 thoughts in seconds. Our goal then is to stop one thought "at the intersection into another thought." Ah, the perfect place—why? Because in between the interruption lies calm, and in the calm, our natural state, we're able to assert our mental power to redirect our resources to our intuition (or Inner Sun), the all-seeing-eye that is constantly aware and knows what's next.

It is *always* within our power to choose *calmness,* and settle our thoughts to "hear" inwardly from our intuition on what will arise next.

So the runner who strained a hamstring and fears a repeat injury can maintain a disciplined mind that won't be pulled into a future that may never happen. Essentially, when we imagine scenarios, we're living them as our reality unnecessarily. Instead, when we perceive difficulty, or an obstacle, rather than allowing our thoughts to wage war, fueled by worry, fear, and defeat (in this scenario, not running again), we can disrupt the thoughts and restore balance.

Sun Tzu is asking us to try, and if we fail, to try again. In the process, you gradually recognize the highest form of self-mastery and discipline is *not* to get deposed by your thoughts, but to usurp them and restore your power at the junction of one thought into the next. Even more skilled is the warrior who can stop the thought at the root—that is, even before it even happens. Without action, we can lose the war, or rather, lose our ability to control our thoughts, instead, swept away in the illusion of our own emotions.

The mastery and art of creating peace in the mind takes practice and discipline.

If you grow angry with your inability to master mental control in your day-to-day experiences, it will only create a "swarm of more thoughts and irritations," and will cause you to lose momentum. Sun Tzu offers a realistic timeline: three months to just prepare the mind, and another three to silence just one thought!

Six months doesn't seem long, not when you think about learning any new skill. Imagine believing you could paint a masterpiece in an afternoon or perfect a jump-shot in five minutes. Even after doing many paintings or a thousand perfect jump-shots, there is always more to learn.

Mastering the mind is a practice, *a way of life*, an art of mastery without resistance so as not to prolong your advancement.

LESSON TWO (7–11): GROWING YOUR CONCENTRATION

Sun Tzu explains that if we bring our mind into a state of concentration, then we will actually gain mastery over both mind and body, and gradually experience Wholeness. We can do this with planning or regulating, rather than living passively, as if we have no control over our future. No matter where we are and what our situation is, we can take one thought at a time and regain control over the life we want to live.

As we assess and strategize our behaviors, we can begin to act as soon as our mind leads us astray. When our mind works hard to distract us from our goal, we will need to regain our concentration. It is a practice. Sun Tzu provides the steps to take to regain equanimity:

- If a thought has taken you away from your center, you should let it go.

- If a thought has taken over or swept your concentration, try not to force it to stop or engage it, but try again later.

It's like if you lose your keys or wallet—your first reaction might be panic and then worry. Your thoughts can easily multiply into hysteria and anger or blame. If you let go of the thought-stream and try again when you're calm, you often find the keys/wallet in a matter of minutes, realizing your original reaction was silly.

Moments like this give you the opportunity to stop the thought at the root, allowing your own intuitive wisdom to discern a way forward to surface—you can restore calm and search within to find the answer effortlessly. But not if your mind is working strongly against you. Instead, it will be difficult to regain control. In fact, you might even grow angrier and more frustrated, and ultimately overwhelmed.

We are the guardian of the mind and we either let our shortcomings win or we grow our concentration to overcome them.

LESSON THREE (12–15): THREE OBSTACLES TO CONCENTRATION

Sun Tzu provides the student-warrior with the three customary ways they might fall to misfortune if pulled from the seat of concentration. The first is when you try to "command" or order your restless mind to act a certain way. You try to force it to stop, but as Sun Tzu explains, the mind can't be ruled by force.

The second way is to try to "govern" it the same way we do our day-to-day life. This might be through bargaining and dictating outwardly what the mind should or shouldn't do, Here again, it is "non-doing," or an effortless-allowing that actually stills the mind.

The last pitfall is to "do" without discernment, to essentially allow the thought to control the body and lead the way without care. This aloofness can seem free, but that is also illusory, because it is impossible to master. Aloofness without discernment is just more habituation.

LESSON FOUR (16–18): FIVE STRATEGIES FOR SUCCESS

To regain concentration and awareness, Sun Tzu gives us five proven strategies to assert control over the senses, which will retaliate and create more war and havoc, until it reaches an uncompromising and incessant state of disorder and unrest. In this warring state, victory will be far away— or very much feel like it.

First, we have to be truthful about how our mind is deceiving us, and then learn when to take action and when not to. In the process, we will begin to watch our thoughts like a battlefield, and know which ones are coming from our intuition (the bridge to our Inner Sun), and which ones are "inferior," or taking us into the mirk of illusion guided by sense and emotion. One is distracting, one *isn't*. To know which is which, we must use discernment and remember to let our unified goal guide our way.

For example, if you're training for a marathon and your goal is to run 26.2 miles without stopping, then that goal will take the mastery of unifying the mind and body toward that outcome. If you're being pulled away from succeeding, you can discern your next action and revise it, so you can continue on with your goal. Equally, you need to keep your senses balanced so as not to pull yourself away emotionally from the goal; make the effort to *not* give any thoughts guided by senses or emotions sway or power to deter you.

Sun Tzu also reminds us that we need to maintain a healthy body to be able to sustain the practice over a lifetime, so our body's limitations won't deter us and distract us further. With a healthy body, we won't be deterred by an ailment.

More specifically, it's asking us to consider how much vital energy we expel through a restless, disquieted mind. Every thought generates and uses energy. The more you are actively connected to thoughts, to people, places, activities, and so on, which use your mind, the more energy you're using and essentially depleting. Even the items in our possession are attached to energy. The more you expel, the more fatigued (and potentially stressed) you become; the more you weaken the body, risk your health or invite imbalances (illness and premature death), the more it will demand rest and give up the will to endure and fight.

Sun Tzu offers strategies to reduce your mental energy use, to keep it in reserve and even build your energy up, to maintain your will and stamina. Then the energy "roads" through the body, which carry this force, will resonate with a strong vital force, giving you a weightlessness, shifting your awareness into the higher centers of the mind (and Inner Sun), providing you with greater awareness.

The five strategies show what will keep us from success, while also demonstrating we can learn our way to victory. In simple words, Sun Tzu is saying that if we know the nature of our mind, we know exactly how we will falter and therefore should never fear any encounter—in this case, encounters are the trials we face everywhere in life.

We can meet any situation, no matter how small or insignificant, with an even mind, dwelling in our seat of mental power that no one, no situation, can stir us from.

FOOTHOLD TO WHOLENESS

Our ability to master the mind begins now. It begins with the next thought rallying for our attention. At first, it can seem that we're very prone to distraction, carelessness, frivolity, and whim, simply because we begin to notice how quick our mind surrenders to thoughts. But we need not be critical of it or the way we've lived, but simply create new strategies to cultivate a new awareness steeped in concentration and trust.

When we trust who we are—that is, we aren't imposed on by others to be better or we aren't listening to self-criticism, but celebrate our inherent beauty and unique inward state—and we resonate with love for our truest nature and gifts, honoring our life, even if we are very far from the path we'd intended, then we will begin to gain footholds into creating a new future, one where we do fully realize our own power and Wholeness.

It starts with becoming aware of one thought, which involves watching, and catching the mind in the act of multiplying thoughts. Emotions, arising from our senses, will also activate us into deeper distraction. But there is hope: we can interrupt the thought-thread when we're in the middle of it. We can become so skilled in interrupting our mind by anticipating what we will say, how we will say it, and the outcome, all at once, and not give it power. We're actually very predictable, thus, we can insert a new pattern through concentration and inquire why those thoughts are pulling us away from success.

Sun Tzu says we can begin to commit to a plan that outwits the mind by meditating on the five principles, which are there for us to cultivate wisdom and discipline. We can utilize them like review questions, which we can ask ourselves at the beginning and end of our day. If we find we have not met the principles, it's okay; we can approach our setbacks with openness and curiosity, not with restraint. We can then review the lessons from previous chapters and see if there are ways to redirect our efforts.

The more aware we are of what we are thinking, and *when* we think it, the more we can address it, and bring our minds into a peaceful state, rather than being in a perpetual war with our immediate surroundings, our body, and the world. We can essentially reach a place where we are aware of what we think, rather than being carried away by it. The more ground we gain (figuratively), the quieter the mind is, and the more our Inner Sun, our intuitive center, is free to guide us.

This is the bridge between the Higher/Lower (perceived) levels of Consciousness; one is an intuitive, inward knowing, the other is dictated by the environment/senses/emotions. Mastery through concentration quiets one, giving power and freedom to the other. In this way, you can cut off worry and fear at the root and regain your power. If the mind takes off, multiplying thoughts, you can assert control again through focused attention. Your mind is already the Master Sun, the enlightened one, right now. So don't be afraid to utilize it and grow your power of concentration, not only when you make special time to meditate, but always: today.

Remember, *your life* is your ceremony and practice. If you're routinely seesawing between awareness or unconsciousness, learn to train your mind to regain Concentrated-Awareness. In the end, because we know ourselves, our reactions, and resistances so well, we can continue to plan and take action to prevent failure and stay the course to achieve Peace and Wholeness.

Begin right now by growing attentive to what is draining your vital energy and start cutting ties. When you stop regarding those outward things as more important than your inward state, you can "call" your vital force back to you, to recharge. Don't feel guilty if you stop thinking about certain people or situations that you normally would. The more you can "cut ties" with the things in your life depleting your stamina and will, the more vitality you'll have to use toward your own goals and future.

Try it. Begin by reviewing your day with all of the times you spent thinking about things that were not necessary or time-wasters. Plan to give that time over to quiet reflection or another practice that will recharge you, like walking or crafting, which can invite mental stillness and concentration.

THE THIRD STEP ON THE HIDDEN PATH TO PEACE AND WHOLENESS

1. Apply the Hidden Path to Peace and Wholeness in whatever way best reveals itself to you without resisting change through a conscious plan of action.

2. Undertake strategies to get at the root of your thoughts in order to master them, so that your disquieted mind is more often in a unified state, rather than a divided one. In doing so, you will conserve energy and maintain your mental seat of power to advance your goals in life.

3. Keep your mind in a state of awareness as the next moment arises, to maintain a strong will and to avoid overwhelm. If you do experience disorder, reestablish your calm.

Undertake by Stratagem is the third step on the Hidden Path to Peace and Wholeness. When we consciously plan for the next moment, we can anticipate how we will react and maintain equanimity.

The mind is trainable—the practice of strategy prepares us to strengthen our will and our efforts.

Planning will give us an advantage, unlike those who don't plan and let the mind wander carelessly; thus, we can achieve our own victories in each instance.

Ruminations: Undertake by Stratagem

*"Confront your mind's resistance when working with thoughts;
do so in a way that does not insinuate fault, but rather approach
them with inquiry."*

– Chapter 3

1. In your daily practice to gain control of busy thoughts or emotions, do you find you are obstinate to making changes? How can you be gentler when it comes to working with reoccurring or strong thoughts and emotions?

2. Sun Tzu suggests that the simple act of preparing the mind can take up to three months—and another three just to silence *one* thought. Does this encourage your practice or do you feel like giving up? If the latter, how can you work on your expectations of your progress?

3. Based on Sun Tzu's teachings, what strategies can you incorporate into your daily activity or practice that would assist you in working through frustration or anger, without being harsh with yourself?

4. Sun Tzu suggests dividing our thoughts and working on them gradually, one at a time, to gain control. Write down three examples of where you know exactly how you will react to a given situation and how you plan to interrupt the thought before it multiplies, to gain greater concentration and fulfillment in your life.

5. What opportunities can you create in your day-to-day life to initiate discernment with each new thought and action, rather than be swept up by emotions/senses?

6. Look at the list of the Five Essentials for Victory, and decide which one seems the best approach to you right now, and why? Which one seems the most difficult, and why?

7. Why do you feel impatient or irritated when you can't control your thoughts?

8. Give an example when you lost control of your mind/emotions and didn't even feel yourself? How would you relive that situation today, using Sun Tzu's stratagems?

9. According to Sun Tzu, the highest form of discipline is to not give into the pull of your thoughts. Share a time when you were able to exhibit this type of mastery.

10. When have you felt your whole mind in a state of peace or equanimity? What's keeping you from that state right now?

----

11. In what ways can you promote a healthier body to help you to sustain a long-term practice toward your life-long goals?

----

12. What would it feel like to *not* fear the result of a hundred encounters?

4

CALCULATING ONE'S NATURE

1. Sun Tzu said: the masters-of-old first put themselves beyond the possibility of being defeated or deterred (when battling for control of the disquieted mind), then worked toward vanquishing all distractions, knowing they would not fail.

2. To be invulnerable against uncontrolled thoughts/emotions lies in our own ability to know the mind.

3. Thus the average student can make themself unaffected by uncontrolled thoughts/emotions but cannot be certain of success.

4. Hence the saying: *victory over the mind can be anticipated, but not forced.*

5. Precautions can be taken to ensure success, and lies in one's ability to guard the mind.

6. When a student possesses a strong will, they will work on the disquieted mind; when the student's determination is weak, they will be overwhelmed by the disquieted mind.

7. The weak-willed student will attempt to hide away in the material world, rather than work on dismantling the ego; the strong-willed student will undertake the path toward Wholeness. The first will shield themself from making progress; the latter will move closer to success.

8. To dwell or remain in a state of expectation will not help you exceed your own understanding of the mind.

9. Neither is it the height of greatness if your ego is given over to praise.

10. Nor is it a sign of mastery to remain attached to the wonders you experience during higher states of consciousness.

11. What the Old Ones called a wise student is the one who not only masters their mind beyond all distractions but does so with little effort.

12. Hence, the student's victories (over the mind) bring them neither reputation for wisdom, nor credit for courage.

13. The student succeeds through unerring efforts. This will give them confidence and certainty (or understanding) to master the mind: *to conquer the mind is to understand there was nothing to conquer.*

14. Hence, the skilled student remains vigilant; they won't allow themself to be put into a position that would tempt them and deter their success. Equally, they will continue to engage in practice until they have reached full mastery.

15. Thus it is when observing: the *successful* student never strives for an outcome while the *unsuccessful* student strives toward and forces a particular outcome.

16. The complete (or Whole) student cultivates awareness and strictly adheres to organization and discipline (in practice); thus, it is in their power to control and achieve success.

17. In regard to mindful organization, we must first *evaluate our mind*; second, *estimate our weaknesses*; third, *calculate our strengths*; fourth, *bring our (perception of) inner and outer worlds into a state of balance and harmony*; and fifth, *assume mastery.*

18. Each of these is considered a step toward reaching higher levels of con-sciousness: to reach the next step, a student must become skilled in the first.

19. A student who is mindfully organized and succeeds is equal to the weight of a one-pound bag of flour on a scale against a single grain.

20. That is because the onrush of thoughts/emotions within the mind is like the bursting of pent-up waters into a chasm of a thousand fathoms deep. So concludes our discussion of calculating one's nature.

INTERPRETING THE LIVING WISDOM OF SUN TZU

Sun Tzu is asking us to undertake the path of the masters who attuned to a higher state of consciousness by guarding the mind and anticipating their thoughts. This is what is meant by calculating your own nature, so as not to be deceived by it. But don't be fooled by the reference to a lofty, higher state. This simply means, a quiet, regulated mind, achieved in numerous ways, including concentration, as discussed in later chapters.

The more we know our disquieted mind, the more we can anticipate what we will do and decide to stop the thought-threads at the root. Habituated, unconscious thoughts multiply—if you've ever been upset or worried, you will likely have experienced a time-shift, where ten minutes can pass and you're still reviewing an issue over and again, like what you wish you had done or hadn't done or said. Sun Tzu is advocating that if you can calculate your own nature, then you can regain control of it.

The more organized and honest we can be about where we are in the moment, the more we can work toward overcoming difficulties. Our assessment, Sun Tzu explains, is necessary to remain focused and realistic. If we become like a general who, after winning a battle, bathes in the praise, then concentration is lost—and so is the goal. The goal is no longer "winning" the battle, but in the outcome that will bring the praise.

Sun Tzu ends on a disheartening note by reminding that the student that goes the distance is rare. But this is also meant as a challenge: "Which will you be, the single grain or the pound of flour?"

LESSON ONE (1–6): ANTICIPATING YOUR THOUGHTS

Sun Tzu is asking us to make the mind our best friend. To know the mind is to *know thyself*, echoing the singular wisdom left by the Oracles of Delphi in ancient Greece. It's an enduring message meant to prod us toward self-discovery and realization. As we anticipate the next moment, we're establishing a mindset that is ready for battle—"battle" being the next conversation or thought to infiltrate our mind.

Believe it or not, an hour, or even five minutes a day, of concentrated attention, will lessen the distractions caused by the senses. It's liberating to have gaps of silence, to observe the world without thinking, just experiencing it. This isn't a special skill that only masters experience. Anyone who undertakes the strategy of calculating the mind can achieve it.

We have infinite opportunities to *calculate the mind*. As you are walking into a supermarket, you can calculate your nature; using technology, you can calculate your nature; before sleep or eating, while working—no matter where you are, you can bring your mind to a state of calm and then foresee what it will do next, so that you can take action.

For example, if you have ever had a special or important guest, or an elder or a grandparent, at your house for dinner, you've experienced calculating your nature. You will have set the table with meticulous care and perfection; ensured the meal was cooked on time and not overdone; you'll have wanted to ensure your guest was comfortable and received the best portion; you will have been mindful of how you dressed, how you spoke and acted, or what gestures you made—everything you did will have been undertaken with scrutiny, not having wanted to say or do the wrong thing, but to act in an honorable way.

In calculating our nature, in this way, we can live our day-to-day moments with this type of awareness, so that everywhere we go, we're our most unified and harmonious Self. We can attune to our highest mind, the mind of our true nature, the one that is truthful and not hiding or insecure or putting on airs; we can be authentic and speak and act in a way that is gentle, calm, and peaceful.

This is how we guard the mind.

When we do, we don't expel excess vital energy that would tire us out, but build our volition (will), which creates a deep determination to progress toward perfection. In this case perfection suggests that we're acting from our united Self, not hurrying or being distracted, but fully involved with whatever is at hand. Done lovingly, with awareness, we leave nothing undone; we act upon each action with careful perfection, harmony, and balance. Thus, we will never get overwhelmed, and if we are in danger of becoming so, we can attune to and start calculating our nature, thereby anticipating our next thought and moment.

LESSON TWO (7–12): AVOID HIDING AWAY

On the Hidden Path to Peace and Wholeness, the student runs the risk of becoming weakened by the mind's inability to win battles, to be ever-unruly, and remain discordant and distracted. If your determination is weak, you will basically "hide away" in the material world. In so many words, we can be defeated and find the struggle so great that we can easily pick up our old, habitual ways, allowing our outer circumstances to appear greater and remain stronger.

Sun Tzu cautions the student not to give up, nor to become arrogant in assuming that if you begin to see advances, that you've achieved something special or above others, thus, inflating self-importance. We can feel good when these changes come, but the moment we start to make something of it, we risk duality—or the notion that we have done something, gone somewhere, overcome something, and we praise our efforts. Sun Tzu tells us that the old masters looked upon a student as wise when they grew beyond the mind of distraction with little effort. It's tricky: you know you've changed, and yet really you're simply evolving, simply entering the next unfolding of your human experience.

As mentioned, it might feel like you're going up a level, like in a video game, where you find the key to the dungeon and it takes you from level 1 to level 2. You can feel boastful—you might have gained clarity or experienced "wonders" by having brought your mind to a higher state of consciousness. You will feel good having overcome your own limitations— perhaps enough to announce your achievement in an ego-bragging way, even if this is unintended. All of life is a reciprocal relationship with the inner teacher, which means that whatever you say/think is being spoken to your own intuition to act upon.

The saying, "Be careful what you speak," is true in these instances when we're creating a new future with new thoughts. A runner who remarks they have never had an injury may find themselves injured, or the person who kicks a cookie habit and marvels that they couldn't imagine ever eating a cookie again may find themself doing just that at a restaurant! Similarly, a person who has lost a lot of weight might praise the mental discipline it took them to create this change, and then throw out all their oversized clothes, sure of themselves (inwardly or otherwise), only to end up gaining back the weight.

Such occasions when we boast and it backfires may keep us humble, because we're forced to act again to bring our bodies back under the rule of the disciplined mind. If we can do it, we will be less likely to mention it again, having known the difficulty it took to achieve balance. Ultimately, we're always just a thought away from "falling" into arrogance or boasting. Equally, these moments give us empathy for others around us who may have their own difficulties in overcoming their limitations.

The goal is to recognize this reciprocal relationship, this inward teacher, that brings us effortlessly to the next Intuitive-Unfolding, our natural state. The more we see every moment—difficult or otherwise—as an awareness that's evolving, the more we will remain at the center, rather than stopping and starting, advancing and striving. As Sun Tzu counsels, "Hence, the student's victories (over the mind) bring them neither reputation for wisdom, nor credit for courage." In other words, you are no more special because you regulate your mind, nor more courageous than anyone else. You simply "become" aware of your mind and unfold to the next moment.

LESSON THREE (13–20): THE CYCLE OF BATTLES

Our confidence in our ability comes from being steadfast, "unerring." When we persevere through difficulty and obstacles, it reveals our intuitive nature, *always there, always present*, and provides us with a constant stream of pure knowledge. As we calculate our nature, we're "hearing" this more, and we begin to act on it: we become certain in a way that we never did before. We become decisive; our voice, our intuition (Intuitive-Knowing), becomes the loudest voice. Doubt, worry, fear, or fear of the future all dissipate, as we stand in balance and act from this center, and once we see results, we actually let go of the external world (always vying for attention) and go deeper inward.

This, in turn, will bring an understanding that there is nothing to conquer, because you aren't competing with people and circumstances; you recognize you've been warring with the way your mind perceives your life. Going inward, winning battles over the mind, you eliminate the enemy inside and experience harmony. Then when you act or undertake something, you won't seek the outcome externally, but automatically go inward, seeing again that to trust your intuition brought deeper peace to your efforts.

The battle is cyclical. Remember, once you outroot one thought, one habit, one pattern, you move on naturally to the next, until your mind is undisturbed at all times (and to begin with, *more* of the time). So, if you turn unworthiness to courage and are given opportunities to "defeat" unworthiness in your mind, and you show courage and win, you have victory. However, it is one battle, and you'll need to be vigilant for the next opportunity that will offer you another chance to be courageous, until it becomes second nature.

The more you regulate the mind, the more you develop a relationship with an invisible teacher—the *hidden warrior* within—that will use your conscious waking time to overcome your weaknesses, until you become the Master Sun, the one who is whole, who can experience Wholeness with all creation and not be at war with it. We are given opportunities to develop our internal "armies" to overcome the patterns of our life. Win one and we will, in another cycle at another time, be given the chance to rise to it again.

Usually, when we have officially "defeated" our internal enemy, we can experience a shift, or release of energy in our body that is freed, allowing us to regain lost or tied-up vital-energy, that now becomes a new resource to go forward and "fight" another battle, another day. Likewise, you may begin to notice repetitions or patterns that seem to test us and grant us the chance to prove we are more powerful than our physical (illusory) limitations. (Noticing them is an example of calculating the mind!) Once we master these repetitive habits, our will grows stronger than its usual limitations, and we gain a foothold, one that will make you feel like the lesson advances—we step higher up the ladder, so to speak, though internally, our perception is simply shifting to be more akin to our truest nature.

Sun Tzu continues to remind us that we don't need to strive or force an outcome. We're very much taught to compete in our physical world, but as we're inwardly working in harmony with our innate nature, we can allow it to teach, talk, and guide us, and if we do, we will overcome our perceived limitations much easier.

An example might be when you accept a job that is not right for you because you need the money. It could be that you felt unworthy of getting a better job or you based your actions on scarcity. But you made the choice, and even if it was the wrong choice, because you lacked courage, you will stay in the job. Months can go by before you finally end it (years, even), before you recognize the lesson: *if only I had been courageous enough to trust that I was capable of a job that better suited me, I wouldn't have gone through this experience.*

What Sun Tzu teaches is that whether you do or don't take the job is irrelevant—you will learn the thing you need to overcome, regardless. It will keep returning until you do. The more you are aware of the choices you make—anticipating your mind—the less you will falter. You can actually see opportunity and difficulty as equal lessons and shorten the length of time it takes you to learn to master your limitations. In this case, had you said "no" to the job you knew wasn't right for you, trusting your inherent intuition, you would've accessed courage. It would have taken you (figuratively) forward quicker, to a more fitting choice, guided by your intuition.

Lastly, Sun Tzu offers the student-warrior an overview of the cycle taking place in the mind when we begin to assert our Generalship. The mind is organized and we can evaluate it, establish our weaknesses, assess our strengths, then tune into and achieve harmony. But the mind is ever-in-motion, so we often repeat the process.

DETERMINING YOUR OWN NATURE

Sun Tzu provides us very specific steps in order to be "unerring" in our determination to experience Wholeness. As we cultivate our intuition, we're asked to keep vigilant by evaluating the weaknesses and strengths of our mind, consistently, while working toward alleviating conflicts that diminish a natural harmony and unity of being. As you refine your efforts, consider whether you are strengthening the ego with self-congratulation or praise from others. Are you focused on a particular outcome, or are you practicing without restraint?

Go through each of the "mindful organization" steps (17) to calculate your own nature and return to this chapter periodically, as a means of checking up on your progress.

Likewise, Sun Tzu is offering you a way to master your thoughts by calculating your nature without ceasing. You are the warrior on a lifetime journey and your duty to self-mastery is forever. As you start to regulate the disquieted mind, you will maintain awareness automatically. Even with a little effort, you'll see the benefits, so that the notion of "forever" is simply an unfolding, rather than something you're stopping/starting, thereby creating more divisions in your thinking. Awareness becomes as integral as breathing, a sharpness you will come to depend on.

If we calculate our nature effortlessly, with understanding and practice, we will see that our battle isn't with other people or outer circumstances, but with our inward state. This means we are accountable to ourselves. We begin to shift from an outward focus to a new recognition that our battle is within, and we can determine who we are and become.

Often, we are likely to make comparisons with others, as we begin to make and experience changes. Sun Tzu is asking us to be cautious of judgment, as we aren't achieving anything (though it can feel like it), but rather, simply respecting our inherent nature. As our truest nature unfolds, it becomes our internal advocate in all matters. It's like having a constant mentor who will guide us to act with harmony, gentility, perfection, unity, cooperation, and love in all situations.

In doing so, we determine our future and our future thoughts. We reorganize our lives, according to how we think and act, moment to moment. Our conquering of and competition with others dissipates, and a deeper sense of purpose unfolds. We're lighter and eager to continue.

Cycles repeat and we will go to "war" again. We will continue to evaluate, knowing our weaknesses and strengths, which allows us to establish mental harmony and balance, and ultimately achieve victory.

THE FOURTH STEP ON THE HIDDEN PATH TO PEACE AND WHOLENESS

1. Apply the Hidden Path to Peace and Wholeness in whatever way best reveals itself to you to bring about harmony and balance.

2. Calculate your nature in order to anticipate your shortcomings. Notice when difficulty presents itself for you to overcome limitations.

3. Once you reach a victory, continue to evaluate your weaknesses and strengths so that you can bring more harmony and mental balance into your everyday life.

Calculating One's Nature is the fourth step on the Hidden Path to Peace and Wholeness. When we consciously recognize the strength of our inward nature to direct our life, we establish trust and certainty in all we do, which will usher in harmony and peace.

The more we allow our intuition (Intuitive-Unfolding) to guide us, the more we will want to honor our truest nature, never wishing to let anything take us from it.

Like ocean tides that ebb and flow, lessons come and go, and we progress, effortlessly to victory.

Ruminations: Calculating One's Nature

"To be invulnerable against uncontrolled thoughts/emotions lies in our own ability to know the mind."

— Chapter 4

- -

1. In what way do you think the mind is trying to *hide away* or *protect* itself? What strategies can you implement into your daily life that will allow you to let go of fears?

- -

2. In what way have you taken precautions to guard the mind, and thus build your confidence and strength of will? How can you remain open and humble to your advancements?

- -

3. When have you experienced a repetitious lesson? Did you learn from it or has it resurfaced (especially by dwelling on it)?

- -

4. If you were to assess the current weakness or limitation that would be most beneficial for you to overcome, which one would you choose, and why?

- -

5. What do you believe is your greatest strength—perhaps something you feel is a gift or your truest nature? Why?—how will you act on it and nurture it?

6. What practice can you bring into your life that would help you evaluate your mind, your patterns, and habits on a regular basis?

7. Describe a time when you forced an outcome and the subsequent results. What would it have taken for you to trust your intuition more the next time?

8. What ways do you feel you are organized and actively working with your mind? What methods can you improve upon?

9. Describe a time you remember being extra vigilant (of your thoughts/emotions) during a situation and it paid off. Or describe a time when you wished you had been more vigilant. What can you do next time to create a different outcome?

10. Describe a time you trusted your intuition and the results.

11. How do you attune to your intuition (Intuitive-Knowing) and trust it?

12. What does your external, day-to-day life look like when your intuition is in harmony and balance?

5

ROOTED CONCENTRATION

1. Sun Tzu said: the control of very powerful thoughts/emotions/senses is the same in principle as the control over the weaker ones: it is merely a matter of separation.

2. Undertaking to calm very powerful thoughts/emotions is not at all different than working with weaker ones: it is merely a matter of organization and selection.

3. For your whole mind/consciousness to withstand the onslaught of thoughts/emotions/senses and remain unshaken—this is affected by indirect and direct action.

4. It is through identifying the weak and strong points of each thought/ emotion.

5. In all efforts to master the mind, direct action may be used to engage thoughts, but the indirect action will be needed to secure success.

6. The student capable of applying indirect actions is as inexhaustible as Heaven and Earth. Indirect action allows thoughts to ebb and flow, without restriction: unending as the flow of rivers and streams. It is like the sun and moon that ends only to begin anew; like the seasons that pass but return once more.

7. There are so few musical tones, yet the combinations of them give rise to more melodies than can ever be heard.

8. There are so few primary colors, yet in combinations they produce more hues than can ever be seen.

9. There are so few cardinal tastes, yet combinations of them yield more flavors than can ever be tasted.

10. In philosophical battle, there are no more than two methods of undertaking concentration of the mind—direct and indirect; yet these two in combination give rise to an endless series of practices.

11. Direct and indirect actions lead on to each other in turn. It is like moving in a circle—you never come to an end. Who can exhaust the possibilities of their combination?

12. The onset of indirect action will even clear away the most powerful thoughts from the mind—like the rush of a torrent, which will roll heavy rocks along in its course.

13. One's decision of when to use indirect or direct action is like the well-timed swoop of a falcon that strikes and kills its prey.

14. Therefore, the good student will be unhurried in their approach and prompt in their decision.

15. Action (or the mind with fixed/rooted concentration) may be likened to the bending of a crossbow, the decision to release the trigger.

16. Amid the turmoil and tumult of the mind there may seem to be disorder and yet no real disorder at all; amid the mind's confusion and chaos, your mental balance may seem to be without head or tail, yet it will be proof against defeat.

17. Simulated disorder brings forward perfect discipline; simulated fear brings forth courage; simulated weakness brings forth strength.

18. Hiding order beneath the guise of disorder is a matter of decision: one who conceals courage underneath timidity assumes they have an endless supply of vital energy to take action. Masking one's strength with weakness suggests one is affected by one's calculating nature.

19. Thus, the student who is skilled at keeping the mind active maintains deceptive appearances, allowing their thoughts to circle back and retaliate; they sacrifice something that their thoughts will seize on to.

20. By baiting the mind to engage, they keep the mind active and busy; then the onslaught of thoughts will get a foothold to rush in.

21. The clever student looks to the consequences of combined control and does not require too much from individual action. Hence, their ability to pick out the right instance to utilize combined action.

22. When utilizing combined action, the student can combat the flurry of thoughts/emotions. *For it is the nature of thought to remain motionless unless prompted, unless allowed to pass by freely, and end on its own.*

23. Thus, the control developed by good concentration is like the momentum of a round stone rolling down a mountain thousands of feet high. This ends the subject of rooted concentration.

INTERPRETING THE LIVING WISDOM OF SUN TZU

To master the disquieted mind, Sun Tzu provides the tool of concentration as a means to establish equanimity and remain mentally unseated by thoughts, senses, and emotions. If we utilize and strengthen our inherent concentration, thoughts will ebb and flow like ocean waves: sometimes the tide will be strong, other times weak, but during *all seasons*, we can keep our mental stamina firm in rooted concentration, and not be knocked over.

Sun Tzu explains the different types of thoughts that will arise and how they will *splinter*, and seem to surround us, so much so that we're more apt to be overwhelmed and give up, like an army retreating.

As we establish rooted concentration, we can delineate the truth of our thoughts, to see them without two sides (dual), but as one *whole expression*, one perception that we call life, our journey. If we make the shift, we can conceive all experiences as equal, rather than through a lens of duality (e.g., difficult, easy). We are the sole decision-maker and orchestrator that discerns reality, thus, we're also the ones who can set ourselves free.

LESSON ONE (1–14): COMBATTING DUALITY OF THOUGHT

To establish a rooted or fixed concentration, we can begin to (immediately) recognize how we separate our thoughts to create duality. Duality—good/bad, right/wrong, happy/sad, pretty/ugly, opportunity/difficulty—creates a hierarchy in our mind and establishes how we will act in any given situation. Since we're more often trained to perceive and want only "good" thoughts, then when a "bad" one comes along, we get overwhelmed (overthrown) and can experience a depletion in our willpower because of the onslaught of emotions that comes with what we deem difficult or uncomfortable.

It is within our power to evaluate thought (good/bad and so on), so we are very much in control of how we will feel in any given moment. Sun Tzu is asking us to be *conscious* of how we label experience through polarity, and identify weak from strong thoughts, and then to actively engage them to determine their truth and their authority over our emotions, to experience them as equal. Equal experience brings harmony; it restores our power as the master creator of the unfolding present moment (or reality).

To combat the mind's perception of duality, Sun Tzu introduces the technique of mastering indirect and direct awareness of a thought's hold over the body, mind, and emotions. If we're attentive, we can readily see how one thought will create other thoughts and emotions, like an army that has set you in a trap and surrounded you, bringing about your defeat. Sun Tzu wants us to surround the thought, so we can learn more about the enemy-of-thought (and its allusive or indirect nature). In doing so, we'll be less likely to be overtaken by it.

To illustrate: if you went to the store to pick up supplies and ended up stuck in a checkout line that delayed you thirty minutes, you could easily succumb to frustration and anger. That is the direct thought that you can immediately dispel. But more often, without fixed concentration, we become unseated and allow more circuitous thoughts to splinter off from the initial one. In this example, the initial thought might be anger or frustration, even impatience.

Then, the circuitous thought will, unwatched, engage you in a feeling of being unlucky, or that the world is against you—*of all the lines to have picked, you chose the slow one!* You can easily upend your day, ushering in the emotions of not being good enough to deserve a day where everything goes right, and you become the target for such difficulty. But guess what? You are essentially determining the thought of whether the day is good or bad—your mind is establishing if the wait is frustrating or not or reminding you the world is against you.

If you were to investigate your thoughts, as Sun Tzu advises, by circling them, you'd discover that the thoughts are not real or concrete but passing—or more specifically—changing, depending on the next arising thought. You could just as easily be in a line and perceive the delay as a godsend, a gift, one you can enjoy. You can take a rest and breathe; you might strike up a conversation with someone else; or inadvertently avoid an accident elsewhere. The delay can become an honored moment to notice you're alive and able to stand and wait.

In the end, you can and must always see the circular nature of dual perception in order to guide the mind to the victory of balance. You very much determine how you view each situation, which is really not one way or the other, depending on how you decide, but unimpeded or uninfected. Only the thought dictates the emotion, and the next thought can determine change or a new reality, *with the conviction of an unseated will.* The more we create and assign duality of opposites (e.g., *this* or *that*, versus what simply *is*, or *whole*), the more we will seesaw and create our own suffering (and future of suffering), as we mentally strive to and fro through the battlefield of emotions.

We can always let go of an either/or mood or thought at war with its surroundings. Sun Tzu is asking us to surround the thought, to prevent it from sprawling or invading into our usual peaceful kingdom, by not letting it rule our action/reaction. If we meet each moment with balance, neither being one way or the other, then the thought will ebb and flow without it creating or stirring up more emotions.

LESSON TWO (15–23): SHIFTING YOUR PERCEPTION

As we recognize the two methods—awareness of the direct thought that is initially unseating us, and then the indirect/circular ones surrounding us and making us overwhelmed—we can choose a strategy to see the truth of the "battle," the truth of the thought fooling us into believing we're helpless. Sun Tzu explains, all actions are connecting us in an infinite circle: bad or good, we decide how we will interpret the next unfolding moment.

If you've ever said, "Here we go again," you can be sure that you've created a long string of habitual thoughts and reoccurring circumstances that seem to intentionally vex you; if you could root your concentration long enough to investigate why these thoughts cause your emotions to rise, and why you deem the circumstance "negative," you could win the battle by shifting your perception to see that only you and your mind determines it so, as its own reality. Thoughts are neutral, and if we recognize how we create the judgment and objectivity associated with them, then we can overcome their power.

We go around in a circle because our mind, stirred by emotion, determines our response. When we reach victory with a goal, for example, we can often look back and realize that every encounter, every situation/thought— worry, fear, courage—every conversation led to the Whole. Often what we felt as resistance and difficulty, or failing, were the moments we chose to believe ourselves incapable of something, or that we deemed as being difficult, rather than just another evolving step in the Whole.

This is the wisdom behind the popular saying attributed to Lao Tzu, that *a journey of a hundred steps begins with a single step*. Meaning, a single action conceived of the mind is connected to hundreds of incremental experiences, even connected to other people, that cannot be fully fathomed (in ordinary consciousness). To make a cup of tea, for example (one step) is connected to everything in the universe. Likewise, one thought generated in the mind can create a lengthy chain of thoughts that is never-ending.

Yet when the mind is at peace, you are no longer experiencing reality with difference (or duality), but allowing it to unfold effortlessly. Then thoughts ebb and flow, and all phenomena, all moments, become one moment. This awareness allows you to relax; you aren't in a hurry; you don't need to strive or be elsewhere. You relinquish the idea of an *over there* that's better; you recognize the delay in the store is perfect and remain in control. Unbound to think, you can actively decide, rooted in concentration, to abide with ease.

Action is effortless, because no matter which way you go, you know the outcome is perfect. You see disorder/order equally; you see confusion and chaos as the circular path to calm; your practice is in balance, no longer fighting with yourself. All that arises will be met as another moment to exercise your perfection. Each new moment is an opportunity that allows you the chance to exercise greater discipline, courage, and strength.

But be mindful and alert. Sun Tzu reminds us that we can pretend we have mastered our thoughts and emotions, when really, we're hiding or suppressing them and have not really changed (the topic of the next chapter).

All can be well, but if you hide your emotions away, or falsely act humble when you're arrogant (or any other dual emotions), you deceive yourself, and in turn, the mind (your intuitive Self) will keep cycling on. More thoughts will inevitably arise to test you. Rather than experience Wholeness, you'll continue to engage more (mental) battles to win or lose in order to establish the kingdom of peace within.

ESTABLISHING YOUR ROOTED CONCENTRATION

How do you begin to establish rooted concentration? According to Sun Tzu, one thought at a time. We don't have to go far to see that one thought can create a disturbance or imbalance that can last hours, days, weeks, or a lifetime. But with a little effort, when you begin to exert concentration—that is, a gentle-awareness and presence, moment to moment—this will become more natural for you, and you will long for it, and achieve it with ease.

The judgment we assign to thoughts creates our circumstances. At first, it might seem difficult to recognize how our mind is winning battles to fool us into believing our emotions and perceptions are firm/concrete and the law. But the only law is our ability to assert our own mental power over the next moment. We are rarely mental lawmakers, but enslaved to the illusion our mind creates when it labels or forms an opinion.

For example, a lost job can be an opportunity over a loss; an injury can be a moment to learn compassion for the Self over a setback—or provide much-needed time to rest from overwork; and failure can redirect our passion along a new road that we might not otherwise have taken. In all three examples, we can eventually grow to a mental state of balance, one that does not include an either/or, but a place suspended in neutrality or Wholeness—we live the moment no longer on a mental seesaw, disturbed by external circumstances, but indwelling from our seat of concentrated attention, our Inner Sun, unimpacted by it.

Each of us has a different life to live and experience, and what we learn, how we shift perceptions, will also differ. Each moment allows us a chance to undertake a strategy to recognize all our individual (perceived) limitations, to call them out into the open, and to work on them one at a time. One thought, one emotion, is more often connected to others, so when we work on one, Sun Tzu's asking us to be aware of the others too, and to address them, and not hide away or be fooled.

As you begin to watch your mind and see what thoughts pull you into limitation, you can investigate them to release the perception of duality and reestablish your own Wholeness. It doesn't take time, so much as it is a matter of willingness to be honest—to recognize when you have dug in and believed a perspective and opinion as the only way to see it, thereby creating your own struggle and striving.

For a day or a week, write down all the times you experience difficulty. Investigate why you feel this way. Look at the initial thought and the corresponding ones that circle it or are even tied to the past. What do they tell you about the things you've chosen to believe about yourself and life (reality) in general? How can you undertake a strategy to essentially see the Wholeness of each situation: if you are choosing happy, it will be happy; if you choose sad, it will be sad. But they are neither, only one *whole* moment, unfolding into the next.

We need not be swayed one way or another, or believe we will be devoid of emotion *if we abide in the unfolding* of the infinite present that's not labeled. Instead, we evolve and unfold; we begin to live effortlessly and in harmony with our surroundings, without an outcome. In doing so, we gain victory. We become unmoved regardless of the situation. Then we can know a new kind of peace and unity.

Rooted concentration is vital to our success. It strengthens our volition (our will) to participate with the Constant-Knowing, to create the next moment, and whether we perceive it or not, it is actively creating the world around us.

Our awareness then, our ability to be rooted in concentration means that every situation that arises can be met with resilience and mastery. It need not make us "risen to emotion," but can remind us to remain in harmony, in order to carry out the next congruent moment.

THE FIFTH STEP ON THE HIDDEN PATH TO PEACE AND WHOLENESS

1. Apply the Hidden Path to Peace and Wholeness in whatever way best reveals itself to you in order to establish rooted concentration right now.

2. Recognize opportunities, moment to moment, to remain or establish rooted concentration, allowing your thoughts to ebb and flow like the tides. If your concentration falters, don't criticize yourself or give in to failure, which will further multiply the enemy-of-thought.

3. Notice encounters where you restrict your emotions or hide them away in pretense that you've mastered them, and instead call the emotions/ thoughts out and address them. Be mindful of feeling arrogant in your advancement, which can act as another false victory.

Rooted Concentration is the fifth step on the Hidden Path to Peace and Wholeness. Never give up or tire of establishing a deep focus in all that you do. The more you direct your will toward perfection and harmony, the more you will be surrounded by it.

Ruminations: Rooted Concentration

"The good student will be unhurried in their approach and prompt in their decision."

– Chapter 5

1. Choose a time when you experienced a (perceived) negative emotion (for example, anger, frustration, fear), and investigate the other side— turn it around, to see it from a positive or neutral way. It's like when two sides fight in a war, both believe they are right. How can you gain a new understanding to see there are *not* two sides, but only one (Wholeness)? Use your experiences and investigate the outcomes.

2. Choose an event that happened to you today and describe it in detail, especially what you thought and how you reacted. Afterward, circle all of the times you can identify that you perceived the experience in a dual way. Going forward, how can you perceive your experience as being whole?

3. What strategies can you establish for your future that will allow you to have deeper concentration? For example, if planning to visit a family member who stirs your sense of unworthiness, how can you investigate the emotion to see it is generated within, unseating your power?

4. At the end of your day, take time to review moments you allowed your thoughts to effortlessly come and go without stopping or trying to rid yourself of them. How did you feel afterward?

5. Today, what thoughts/emotions did not rule you, but returned frequently to try to get your attention again? How did you handle them—with concentration, or were you pulled from your seat of (mental) power?

6. Share a time when your initial (direct) thought/emotion triggered an overwhelming number of other thoughts/emotions? What did you do in the past to alleviate the situation, the feeling of being overwhelmed (or helpless)? What can you do in the future?

7. When our thoughts impact us directly or indirectly, which one is easier to recognize? How will you begin to see both as a unified method of maintaining your concentration?

8. Consider what it means to you that action is soft and moving, like a bending bow? How can you establish less resistance to circumstances?

9. When have you experienced a period of chaos or disorder, only to look back and be thankful for the experience—that, no matter how "bad" it seemed, it was ultimately beneficial? How can you continue to win victory by seeing all difficulty as an unfolding opportunity?

10. Sun Tzu reminds us not to be deceived by circular thinking, and not to let our mind get carried away, or "seize" onto any one tangent. Name and take responsibility for a time today or this week when you fooled yourself into thinking you engaged proactive thoughts, but in fact, just prolonged the "battle."

11. At the end of today write down the thoughts that are still preoccupying your mind. Sun Tzu reminds us that when we hold onto the thought (make it motionless), it keeps ruminating and causes a war. In contrast, if we can let it go, it will pass. Try it now. Report the results.

12. Sun Tzu likens good concentration to "a round stone rolling down a mountain thousands of feet high." List the moments you displayed a level of rooted concentration and let the thoughts roll off.

BALANCING WEAK AND STRONG POINTS

1. Sun Tzu said: the student whose mind is waiting and ready when the enemy-of-thought arrives will be full of energy to take it on; the student who is late to mental battle will arrive exhausted.

2. Therefore, the clever student imposes their mental will on the enemy-of-thought but does not allow the thought/sense-emotion to be imposed on them.

3. Thus, the student who controls the flow of mental thoughts will make it impossible to be controlled by them.

4. If the mind (volition) is lazy, the clever student can easily invade the disruption with concentration, thereby starving the mental flow of thoughts from further action (or multiplication); if the mind is rooted in distraction, the student can evict the mental flow of thoughts.

5. Asserting strong will and concentration while letting thoughts pass without engaging, will keep the mind fluid, evolving (unfolding), like an army on the go that can't gain a foothold to attack the kingdom.

6. The mind that flows effortlessly without engaging in thought will keep it from engaging in ideas/emotions that would otherwise naturally stop, deter, or cause the student to suffer.

7. The student can be sure to succeed in maintaining mental balance (equanimity), if they allow their thoughts to flow unrestricted. With a strong will preserving Wholeness, the mind is like an army holding its position, making it impossible for the enemy to attack.

8. Hence, the student is skillful in recognizing those thoughts that are weak and can be easily let go of, while also being ready to acknowledge when a thought is beginning to take root (attack) and establish a mental foothoid.

9. *Oh, the art of subtle mental disturbance and distraction!* Through you, we learn to keep our mind unmoved, unimpacted, and hence, we can hold your fate in our hands!

10. You may advance and multiply in our minds, to the point we find it irresistible to keep thinking incessantly, especially when you attract our weak points, our emotions, and desires. You can advance so fast that we get carried away and cannot catch you.

11. If the student wishes to stop the mental flow of thought—the upheaval and disorder of thinking—they can immediately engage concentration, no matter how far gone the overwhelm seems. All they need to do is focus elsewhere, to shift the train of thought onto something else, and the conscious mind will follow.

12. If the student is too weary to regain concentration, they can prevent the mind from continuing its "battle" or mental tirade—those moments when it seems impossible to think of anything else—simply by throwing something odd and puzzling at it to slow it down, divert it.

13. By discovering the mind's nature and remaining in a state of deep concentration that is unmoved, we can keep our attention rooted, while actively dividing the thought-threads.

14. The student can utilize concentration to approach the thought-chain that has its attention and begin to divide it into factions. Hence the concentration which is whole, can now address the thought-chain which is separate, and therefore weak, gaining an advantage.

15. And if the student is able to conquer the "small" or inconsequential thoughts with deep concentration, allowing them to pass unrestricted, the student will gain a foothold of peace; the enemy-of-thought will not win.

16. The mind that is effortlessly-unfolding without giving up its position—that is, dwelling in the past or looking to the future—will maintain its calm and peaceful state, as it won't allow a thought to take root for too long, whereby it could multiply and create mental disorder.

17. For if the mind stays too long in one place, the student invites an invasion of thoughts. Likewise, if the mind remains flexible, never staying on one thought too long, then it strengthens the whole will. If at any time, the mind splinters with rushing thoughts, the conscious mind will find it difficult to engage concentration, which acts as a type of reinforcement, and risks being overthrown into a chaotic mental war.

18. If the student-warrior can expel disquiet from the conscious mind, they can maintain equanimity, rather than allowing any thought to weaken their resolve/will.

19. Knowing our mind, and how easily it is led into a mental war with our surroundings, we can root our concentration without ever having to engage.

20. But be mindful, for if the mind is flitting to one place and you attempt to bring it under control, and then, before you can, it flits to another place and then another, no matter how you attempt to bring the splintered, disquieted mind under control, you won't be able to—your mental concentration will be weakened in many places. It would've been better had you maintained your mental center and attacked each thought as it arose!

21. Through experience, the student should know that even if the thoughts or sense-emotions seem to exceed the power of their rooted concentration and appear impenetrable, they are not. Victory over the conscious, restless mind *is* possible.

22. Though the thought-threads appear to be stronger in number, you can prevent them from multiplying further. It takes cunning and cleverness not to be overtaken mentally, and to prevent the thoughts from multiplying and escalating through inquiry.

23. Rouse your restless mind so you can see clearly what is sweeping your concentration away, and find the vulnerability of thought, which has no true hold on you.

24. Carefully compare your disordered mind with the one that is rooted in concentration, for both are indwelling simultaneously, and you will see which is strong and which is naturally weak.

25. In assessing the nature of the mind, recognize that your power lies in reasserting your center, your deep concentration that is unwavering. When you restore peace and balance, the mind will be clear and new thoughts will not so easily arise.

26. How victory is achieved is through these "battles," through interrupting the thoughts and sense-emotions, which come and go in cycles, but can essentially be conquered if you are willing not to be overthrown, and continue to learn to master them.

27. All student-warriors can see the way their mind tries to create mental disharmony, conquering the conscious mind and enslaving it. But what no one realizes is that this awareness of how the mind works (and battles) is the very thing that will create victory and Wholeness.

28. Do not repeat your bad habits once you have identified them, especially if you have won a victory over them. Rather, apply the method which gave you victory over yourself to your next circumstances.

29. Mental battles are like water that runs its course naturally from high to low places, unrestricted.

30. So in the battle for mental calmness and composure, the way to avoid being overrun by strong thoughts is to allow them to flow unrestricted, where they will remain weak and pass away, not taking root or multiplying.

31. Water shapes its course according to the nature of the ground over which it flows: likewise, the student-warrior establishes an enduring victory through a continual effort that establishes the rule of calm and harmony in the mind.

32. Therefore, just as water retains no constant shape, the whole mind (conscious-unity) has no restrictions or limits; it is boundless.

33. The student who can modify their habits and assert a strong will over the restless, disquieted mind, will succeed in becoming whole and dwell in equanimity; such a student is in accord with their Inner Sun.

34. Be warned: the conscious mind is ever-changing. Just as the seasons are not permanent but evolving, one into the next, so too will the mind's perceptions also evolve, experiencing great growth and expansion, and conversely decrease and diminish. The wise student will do well to remain bending and flexible no matter the season.

INTERPRETING THE LIVING WISDOM OF SUN TZU

Sun Tzu is asking us to consider the importance of maintaining a flexible mind. The moment we try to restrict the flow of thoughts that would otherwise naturally pass, they will begin to take root. The good news is that even if our restless thoughts do take root and begin to multiply, creating an endless thought-chain, we can still regain control, through concentration, and bring our mind into a balanced state, no matter how difficult it seems.

Each of us knows what situations, people, and circumstances will trigger our reactions: we can essentially predict ahead of time what we will think in every given situation. Rather than allow ourselves to be carried away, Sun Tzu is advocating that we interrupt the flow of thought, thereby making it less rooted; we can go as far as diverting our attention to something odd or ridiculous to stop the progression of thoughts from advancing like an army that will camp and continue to lay siege to our peace and mental calm.

The more we investigate our thoughts, break them up, make the thought-threads smaller, the more they'll be reduced in power. But we must be attentive: if our mind is flitting around from place to place, we can easily risk overwhelm and mental fatigue, and give up. Even though it may seem like our restless thoughts are winning, they're actually giving us the opportunity to learn about the way we think and essentially, through regulation, become the very thing that liberates us.

The softer we are in our approach by effortlessly allowing our thoughts to pass without hindrance, the more we will return to a state of equanimity and maintain it.

LESSON ONE (1–8): KEEPING THE MIND IN A FLUID STATE

Sun Tzu is offering us expert advice on the method of balancing the weak and strong points of our minds. To begin, we can meet every moment that is unfolding in a gentle way, without mental restriction or judgment (which creates duality) and instead, remain very open and fluid. If we are ready, observing our thoughts, and actively allow them to unfold, without restriction, we will have the energy to *bend* into the next moment. However, if we're meeting the next unfolding moment late (reactively), then we will grow mentally fatigued and not be as malleable, and risk losing our mental calm.

When we assert our will (volition) and apply rooted concentration *in the moment*, our thought-tangents can't gain a foothold into our peace, like an army attacking the boundary of a kingdom. The more we can keep our mind in this fluid state, the less likely we will be to fixate on a thought and allow it to have a hold over us. Our success depends on the free flow of thoughts: grab onto one of them (focus on it) and it will "attack" or disrupt our mental balance.

So, we're learning the skill of recognizing which thoughts are weak and which are strong, or which ones will disrupt us, and gain strength to overpower us, and which ones won't. Our goal is always to maintain balance, so that a weak thought cannot become strong and take over the kingdom of the mind.

LESSON TWO (9–16): GETTING TO KNOW YOUR STRONG AND WEAK POINTS

The disquieted mind is very subtle in distracting us. For starters, we assume our thoughts are something we can point to, within our head (or brain), but they're essentially boundless, occurring in the "field" of perception. At the same time, our intuition, equally boundless, exists as part of this (figurative) field. You can sense your limitless intuition, or get a hint of it, when you "hear" or mentally sense someone is about to call you, demonstrating how easily it can tune in to another's energy, in the field, free-flowing past the mind or body.

Furthermore, our thoughts, as they occur, are essentially a natural process, and not something we need not vilify or be rid of. Thoughts are naturally occurring, and we can remain open to this process with inquiry and awareness. Each arising thought offers the framework to remain in a state of equanimity, to be unmoved and unimpacted, creating a new state of awareness no longer enslaved like a prisoner of war, but unhindered by them.

Gradually, our mind (or awareness) empties, the noise stops, and an inward presence is felt... in the beginning, you might interrupt this calm-quiet, as you notice you actually stopped thinking! But that quiet, that peace, is the true norm. Yet untrained, the mind simply reacts and gives into habits. According to Sun Tzu, the more you can settle your disquieted mind and "conquer" its habits, the more its power will recede and over time, relinquish control, giving way to serenity and peace.

If you have ever had the experience that felt like your mind was "running away from you," or "taking over," then you will understand how irresistible it is to repeat and replay the same thought time and again—we can actually not even notice that this is happening. If it does, Sun Tzu is advocating that you focus elsewhere, and no matter how far embedded the thought is, to "shift the train of thought onto something else." If you do, the thought will stop and the conscious mind will follow.

If your disquieted mind is thinking incessantly, for example, and you were to focus on the breath (a common calming technique), the conscious mind will follow. It may take several tries to redirect the mind from the grip of a thought-thread, but with concentration it is possible. You could even throw something really odd or puzzling at the mind to slow it down.

This is how you get to know your weak and strong points, and can establish your mind's equanimity, its truest nature. Once you regain concentration, you will still circle around to the thought-thread and can work on dismantling its hold, a piece at a time, until it loses its power and you are back in charge. If you can manage the small, inconsequential thoughts, allowing them to pass without holding on to them or giving them more strength, making it more likely that you'll maintain your mental calm.

LESSON THREE (17–24): THE FLEXIBILITY OF THOUGHTS

Sun Tzu is showing us that the disquieted mind that generates thoughts, over peace, can remain flexible to maintain its free or empty state with each unfolding moment. But as soon as we allow our mind to stay in one place, on one thought, we're inviting an "invasion of thoughts" that can easily splinter to many thoughts, generating myriad tangents, making them near-impossible to get under control, possibly even creating a very chaotic, disruptive mind.

It is up to the skillful student to bring the conscious mind into balance. The more you know your own mind—the way it will create mini-wars over and over again, running over the same habituated thinking—the more it will create obstacles to your peace. In fact, if your mind flits from one place to another, without concentration, you risk overwhelm. As thoughts easily splinter, causing distraction and disorder to take over mind, you'll need to readily reassert concentration to regain balance.

Sun Tzu is advising never to let it get that far, but to "attack" and assert rooted concentration as soon as strong thoughts arise. The good news is that even if the thought/emotion seems very strong—that it appears impenetrable and there is no way to stop it from overwhelming you—you *can* regain control. It takes cleverness to see each thought clearly, to keep them from multiplying and taking over.

By identifying the weak and strong thoughts that will either pass easily or take root, we can act accordingly and win ourselves victory.

LESSON FOUR (25–28): THOUGHT-CYCLES

We're always in a position to assess the nature of the mind and restore our center through deep concentration. When we do, our mind regains its balance and strength, and so, in general, thoughts are less likely to arise. Our mind works in cycles, and as you establish awareness, you'll gain a foothold into your intuition, your Inner Sun, that acts as teacher and guide for your future and life, and will bring situations that allow you to break through your own limitations.

If, for example, you lack courage or dislike confrontation, over time, and usually in hindsight, you can recognize the subtle external skirmishes that arise and will cause you to either exhibit courage or will shirk from it. You may have lived your whole life very timidly, but with awareness of your thoughts, you can make sound changes and act with courage. Often, we can see the "lessons" or "tests" come in cycles, revealing a pattern.

This is why Sun Tzu also says our thoughts are the very thing that liberate us—these mental battles aren't with the external world, but happening inwardly. They allow us to break the impression that we are weak and confined in a body, because through unity and Wholeness, we are, in fact, boundless and invincible. The more we are attentive to the signs, symbols, and occurrences happening in cycles of our thoughts, the more we can become aware of what we need to do to grow free of them.

The more we recognize the way the mind will create thought-threads that teach us about the way we perceive life and then let them go, the more we can make progress in shifting our perceptions and evolving toward our truest nature. If you happen to recognize that you have found yourself multiple times in situations where you need to assert courage, you will look for the next one. Just like Sun Tzu says, at the opening of the chapter, when a similar situation arises, you will be waiting to engage the thought and react by making a different choice to win a new victory.

Difficulty then becomes opportunity; our restless thoughts become ladders to our limitless nature as we let go of our habitual thinking for a higher level of consciousness—or rather, a mind not straying or being led, but commanding it, like a General! We harness it through rooted concentration.

Sun Tzu states that few students stop to notice this awareness of how the mind works, even though it's the very thing they need to create victory and Wholeness. Yet those who can recognize mental harmony, and the larger cycles of limitation, will bring more awareness to the next "battle." In so many words, when your life is repeating, when you do and say the same things over and over again, you can assert a new Generalship over the mind/thoughts to create a new way forward.

Once you identify the habit and the principal limitation, don't repeat it; work to root your concentration, so you aren't overrun by it anymore. Then, when it happens again, be prepared and don't risk being distracted by the same mental tangent.

LESSON FIVE (29–34): LETTING THOUGHTS FLOW

The thoughts that invade the territory of the mind should be allowed to run their course naturally, just like water runs unrestricted from high to low places. Once we engage a thought and try to suppress or stop it, we give it attention and make it more real and powerful. The more we can let thoughts flow unhindered, the more likely we are to keep our natural state of concentration, free from disruption.

In fact, Sun Tzu suggests that the more you allow thoughts to flow unrestricted, the more you will create a natural state of harmony *more of the time,* and eventually, *all of the time.* The opposite is also true: if you restrict the flow of thoughts, you will get disruption. To achieve a state of calm-balance, we can modify the way we think—the way our cyclical mind asserts a strong possession over our consciousness—to disrupt our natural state of calm.

Sun Tzu ends the chapter with a warning for the student to recognize the cycles, the times when it will seem they are growing and shifting their perceptions and overcoming limitations, and the times when they will be in a state of transition, just like the seasons. As careful Observers, we can recognize the cycles, so we can rest in conscious-unity and maintain balance all the time.

BALANCING YOUR WEAK AND STRONG POINTS

Sun Tzu offers us the knowledge that no matter how deeply rooted your mind gets in a thought-thread, no matter how many times it repeats it, no matter how irresistible it is to think it and get carried away, you *can* overcome it. We don't have to go anywhere or schedule special time to consider the lessons and how we can apply them. The work begins *right now.* We can easily review our thoughts and see what is bothering us and what's not: weak and strong.

Weak thoughts are those that we *can* allow to pass by without much effort; strong thoughts are those that are usually attached to an emotion—

one often long-standing—that have the ability to pull us into one of those endless thought-tangents. Take an inventory of your thoughts, right now, and decide which feel small and which have a greater hold. (In later chapters, we'll assess how weak and strong thoughts appear to us in the field of perception, and how to "battle" them to maintain the harmony of your Inner Sun.)

Sun Tzu is showing us there is hope for a mind that is weak. *Always.* No matter who you are, no matter what you've done in life, no matter how overwhelmed and disruptive or chaotic your mind seems, you *can* be the victor. We're being asked to show up each unfolding moment *ready, aware, and flexible* to allow our thoughts to come and go through rooted concentration.

If we do, guess what? We actually create that sense of unrestricted flow as a new path and gentle way of living (being/becoming). Even a little awareness, of the way a strong thought can hook your focus, can make a difference. The small effort of gentle redirection of your attention, letting a thought pass, can foster a calm mind as a natural, constant state.

What happens if our thoughts get (figuratively) carried away? Sun Tzu is offering us knowledge to use in the field *immediately* to disrupt the thought-thread and break it into small thoughts. Once you interrupt the flow of thought, it stops multiplying. Think of a time someone interrupted you and you couldn't recall what you were saying. Exactly this. Except you're going to do it to your own mind, to keep your focus, interrupt your thoughts, and maintain your centered concentration and calm.

Say, for example, you are at home enjoying a lovely cooked meal on a quiet Sunday afternoon, and the moment you take your first bite, your neighbor decides to make a whole bunch of noise by mowing the lawn, causing frustration to take hold in your thoughts. The emotion might go from weak to strong, and will continue to cycle around and around, because you believe that the neighbor's external action of making noise is invading your mental calm.

Sun Tzu demonstrates how easily your mind will draw you to either reaffirm a limitation—the act that someone is causing you harm—since it's one of the strongest perceptions. But once recognized as such, it can be overcome to create mental freedom. In theory, a person is mowing their lawn. Only the mind/thought decides that it is being bothered by this. It could be that you are the only one noticing the noise (and certainly the person mowing is having their own thought-thread!) Mastery of the mind comes from not battling the (perceived) external world and provoking emotions that will create a seesaw effect, but from remaining flexible, a mind that is rooted in concentration to create Wholeness.

Many of our emotions (especially when we start to become aware of our thought-threads) are rooted in the past, to episodes and experiences already lived. If we were a timid/quiet child, we can easily find ourselves as timid adults too. In the noisy neighbor scenario, the focus can be placed on the inward state of the Observer, not the outward one. Inner creates outer—in theory, there isn't an inner or outer, only a perception or Observer experiencing them as two—and our goal, using Sun Tzu's wisdom, is to interrupt the flow of thought, before we get taken down the proverbial bunny hole into endless emotion and unproductive thinking that really keeps our perception enslaved.

If the situation with the lawn mowing occurred again the next week, the mind-thread would most likely repeat and strengthen. In fact, you can probably pick people/situations in your life that would immediately provoke a thread of habituated mental responses from you. Sun Tzu advocates that if you know ahead of time how you're going to react, you can interrupt the flow of thoughts, splitting up the reactive thread to maintain concentration. We may like to think our thoughts are justified, and they certainly might be; what we often miss is that we actually control the outer world, our experience, through our (inward) thoughts.

If your mind ceased in its deliberations (and grew silent) what would the outer world appear as? Not disruptive, but *still*, at peace.

If we feel a neighbor is a nuisance, they will be, and we will continue to assert this opinion as the ultimate authority and reality, one we feel hopeless to ever overcome and get free of—and certainly, they may *truly* be the definition of noisy, but your reaction, thoughts, and judgment are still yours to control or create a war. Through intuitive guidance, you can remain in peace, centered and unseated.

If instead, we're whisked away by our thoughts, we do have the ability to interrupt the thread to create a different outcome. We love to be right; we love to hear our convictions, and can see, through Sun Tzu's wisdom, that the multiplication of thoughts is going to occur with our supreme focus and fuel. In this way, the world and our emotions become *changeless*, and we cease to evolve to our birthright of freedom and boundlessness. When we decide to not be annoyed by our neighbor (or countless other external disturbances), our history of ideas will no longer be enforced and our world reorders; it can't remain the same.

Sun Tzu is offering us the wisdom to interrupt the thoughts, so that they shrink and are more easily managed. But if that doesn't work, then we're asked to get creative: throw the mind something odd or absurd. For example, if you can't break the hold of the thought-thread on the nuisance neighbor, imagine that there are cows out there making the noise! If your thoughts attempt to root themselves deeper, ready to multiply, think about those cows bumping around and making more noise. They might be mooing, their bells clanging—or they could be blue cows or cows climbing the roof to jump over the moon.

Either way, if you think about the cows, guess what? You interrupt your train of thought (even bring humor to the situation) and can begin to regain your concentration.

Equally, Sun Tzu shows us that mental stillness arises through concentration and attention, which we can master, to recreate our world. When you take the time to establish rooted concentration, you won't be swept up by your emotions or thoughts; you then also begin to master yourself—master your (perceived) limitations. Solutions can appear. Most of all, you will gain a new outlook on life.

Once the nuisance neighbor (in the example) has no impact on you, your life begins to change—and because our lessons on perception often come in cycles, we will most likely see other opportunities to assert concentration over similar situations. Soon, you may find you're not as easily bothered by family members or coworkers either, having made changes to your thought patterns. As you assert your rooted concentration, and maintain mental calm, you'll see no one is bothering you; your mind created that view and you have finally reinterpreted it, and taken back control.

Once you are *free* (of the thought-thread or fixed-reality created by your thoughts), you also free everyone else you involved. In other words, your thought that the neighbor was a nuisance is the only way they have been perceived; free of your thought, they become free to be their natural Self as well. (This goes for any perception you create about the external world.)

As your thoughts change, your perception does too (often through empathy) and the outer world will take on a less separate, more harmonious aspect. Eventually, you may come to recognize that you are shaping the world around you, and if you slip up and become disordered mentally, the outer world will take on this confused perspective also. Likewise, you can also see that your restored calm will also restore a more harmonious world.

Recognize the cycles and the habits you have to overcome; the Inner Sun will be there to guide you. When this happens, it's a very beautiful experience, because it will feel like you have a twin friend working with you, guiding you, wanting your best, and giving you the situations/

opportunities to demonstrate you are without limit. Gradually, as you work in unity, as one whole expression, you become expansive; love floods your whole view.

Over time, you will be glad for your (perceived) difficulties, because you will see that without them, you would never have been aware of your limited impressions. With time, you will also create a mental state that is naturally in flow and balance, in the same way water creates a groove in the Earth as it travels unrestricted. Remember, when you let the mind rule you and carry you unaware, you are only cheating yourself out of living your life without limits.

THE SIXTH STEP ON THE HIDDEN PATH TO PEACE AND WHOLENESS

1. *Apply the Hidden Path to Peace and Wholeness in whatever way best reveals itself to you to bring balance to your weak and strong thoughts right now.*

2. *As the next moment unfolds, recognize opportunities to establish a strong will (volition) rooted in concentration, before a situation that would unseat your power can arise. In doing so, you create the outcome before you have engaged! Truly think about the opportunities that exist to assert your strong will ahead of every encounter.*

3. *Notice situations and thought processes in which you allow the thoughts to multiply, taking you far into "enemy territory" until you are a prisoner. When you identify the thoughts and the emotions that weaken you, you can master your will to remain steady with practice.*

Balancing Weak and Strong Points in the mind is the sixth step on the Hidden Path to Peace and Wholeness. Our habituated thought-threads are not concrete, though it can seem like it. With time, the more we unseat these "enemies-of-thought," the more likely we will discover freedom and a new way of life will open up for us.

Ruminations: Balancing Weak and Strong Points

"The student who controls the flow of mental thoughts will make it impossible to be controlled by them."

– Chapter 6

1. Recall a time today when you allowed a thought to come and go without resistance. What was the thought and why *wasn't* it given a chance to take root?

2. Recall a time today when a strong thought overtook you and caused your mind to feel chaotic and disordered. What caused the thought to take hold?

3. What are the chances the thought-thread from Rumination 2 will occur again in the future? Can you predict how you will react again? If so, what strategy might you try to interrupt the flow of thoughts next time?

4. Can you identify cycles of thought, or moments when it seems like your Inner Sun is teaching you to walk effortlessly on the Hidden Path to Peace and Wholeness?

5. What do you want to change about your life and how might asserting rooted concentration help you create a new way forward?

6. List some creative ways you can interrupt yourself when a thought-thread takes you over.

7. List some creative ways that you can engage your mind to draw on the odd or absurd, so that you can interrupt your thought-processes and regain your center of concentration?

8. Explore the circumstances (people, events) that most often trigger a very deep emotional response. With inquiry, how might you enable an understanding of the part you play in supporting this reality?

9. What will it take to drop the familiar thread-of-thought you know you conjure the next time you see/encounter the people described in Rumination 8? In what ways can you interrupt your usual thoughts?

10. What does it feel like when you have rooted concentration and how might you continue to embrace it as your natural state all the time?

11. Decide on three ways in which you will shift your train-of-thought onto something else during an upcoming confrontation or conversation with someone, to stop your thought-thread from taking root.

12. Give an example of when you have felt free of your own mental thought-thread. What did you like about this?

7

CALCULATED-AWARENESS PRACTICE

1. Sun Tzu said: when observing the mind, the student receives commands from the unobstructed Intuitive-Unfolding.[1]

2. Having gained a footing, rooted in concentration, the student must blend and harmonize the Two Selves (the conscious and intuitive mind) before true mastery can be established.

3. After that, comes maintaining calculated-awareness, which is not difficult, so long as you can turn difficulty into opportunity, misfortune into gain, deviousness into honesty.

4. Thus, once the mind is in a state of equanimity, you see the Gentle-Way is a long and circuitous route, and that there is no end, no goal, but rather a constant evolving.

5. A mind centered in equanimity is advantageous as it is unrestricted by limitation; likewise, an unruly mind given free rein is dangerous.

6. It would be foolish to carry habits and repetitive patterns with you on the long and circuitous journey—you might even think that you have things under control and can deal with them when a mental battle arises, but these deep-set patterns will only weigh you down, making you struggle.

---

1   Pure intuition unobstructed by thought, always present and unfolding.

7. Thus, if you were to command your deep-seated patterns/habits to go, or forced them to stop, hoping to wrestle the advantage and restore your center, you will fail.

8–10. In this scenario, the strongest habit/emotions will be in the forefront of your mind, followed by the sensation of overwhelm and fatigue, while your concentration will be cut in half, and keep you from your goal of a unified and whole mind.

11. It is understood a mind without concentration is lost; further, if you are mentally fatigued, your vital energy will continue to wane.

12. We cannot reach Wholeness—unity of Higher and Lower Consciousness —until we are in harmony with all our thoughts.

13. In fact, we aren't fit to be Master of our mind unless we are familiar with our truest nature and all the highs, lows, pitfalls, obstacles, its hardships, and wanderings.

14. We shall be unable to bring our mind to its natural state unless we make use of our calculated-awareness, which acts as a guide in our conscious life.

15. In mental conflict, practice the art of pretense in which your thoughts are recognized as false impressions, and you will succeed. Take action only if there is a real advantage to be gained.

16–17. Circumstances decide whether to use concentration or dividing your (unruly) thoughts as a form of regaining your mental balance. Be as quick as the wind, so that you can prevent or limit the growth of a mental tangent.

18. Enforcing your will, to regain mental control, be like the ravaging fire, and at the same time as unmovable as a mountain.

19. Let your plans be certain, direct, and impenetrable as the dark of night, and when your thoughts/consciousness moves, assert your will through concentration like a thunderbolt.

20. When you unbuild or "lay waste" to your thoughts, through asserted-will, disunite fleeing thoughts and allow them to disperse; if new thoughts arise, devote the same attention to disbanding them for the benefit of your whole mind.

21. Ponder and deliberate before your consciousness moves (or follows) another thought.

22. The student will conquer the mind who has learned the trickery of thoughts to deviate from the center of Concentrated-Awareness.[2]

23–24. The Book of the Gentle-Way says: in establishing rule over the mind, chanting will not be as effective as gongs or drums; likewise focusing on an everyday object will not be as effective as using a sacred picture or banner.[3] In either case, the ears and eyes of the student can be focused on a particular point (sight/sound).

25. Thus, the Two Selves (the conscious and intuitive mind) can form one united consciousness that will make it impossible for the strongest or weakest thoughts to even form; this is the art of managing many thoughts.

26–27. Then, at night, during practice, make use of sound or focusing on a candle flame. And by day, place sacred pictures or banners in your environment to influence your eyes and ears to maintain focus, because the student's whole mind can be robbed of equanimity.

28. A student's spirit is most acute in the morning; by noon, the mind begins to tire, and in the evening, they are bent on sleep.

29. A clever student, therefore, will have a calmer mind in the morning, avoiding any preoccupation of thoughts, when the spirit is sharp. They will strike—or assert concentration—when the mind is sluggish and inclined to be lazy or in a hurry to sleep. This is the art of studying the mind's moods.

---

2   Concentrated-Awareness suggests a level of concentration that goes beyond ignoring distractions, and withdraws attention fully from the body, senses, environment, to achieve mastery over them, ushering in a heightened state of awareness, by which you are attuned to the guidance of your intuitive source and wisdom.
3   Sun Tzu advises the use of sacred pictures and banners, because they're imbued with higher vibrational qualities, that the student can attune to for support during practice.

30. Disciplined and calm, to await the appearance of disorder and distraction of the mind: this is the art of retaining self-possession.

31. To be near the goal while the mind is calm and at peace; to remain centered, waiting with ease when the thoughts toil/struggle; to remain in deep concentration so as not to feed your thoughts—this is the art of conserving your strength and vital energy.

32. To refrain from interacting with your thoughts when you are calm, harmonized, at peace, and confident—this is the art of contemplating your circumstances.

33–34. Just like an army wouldn't advance against an enemy uphill, nor oppose it coming downhill, do not pursue your thoughts, nor give into the temptation to get angry, should it arise.

35. Do not let the mind bait or tempt you; do not interfere when your concentration returns home (to its center).

36. When you surround a thought, leave it an outlet to go freely. Do not press too hard.

37. Such is the art of mental warfare.

INTERPRETING THE LIVING WISDOM OF SUN TZU

Sun Tzu explains that our mind will create wars to keep us from hearing the pure messages of our inner wisdom. Whether we can sense it or not, our intuition, our inner "voice," is guiding us, like a General giving an army commands. The quieter our thinking-mind is, the more we can attune to our inner truth and be guided effortlessly by it. They go hand-in-hand through the practice of calculated-awareness. As we change our perception from one of duality, to one in favor of unity, we begin to experience our day-to-day lives with equanimity.

How do we welcome this state of mind?

Through recognition of the disquieted mind, which perpetuates the cycle of distraction and disorder that will appear difficult to bring under order. Just like an army that sets out in a formation, that engages and ends up in a haphazard situation, so too, your thoughts scatter, making it seem impossible to bring them under control. With our concentration shattered, we will feel weak and unworthy, wanting to force changes (to make our mind stop its incessant chatter, for example), but will only create more obstacles instead.

Sun Tzu's advice is to employ strategies that strengthen our awareness, which then makes our will stronger, creating an impenetrable wall of concentration and attention. Through it, our intuition unfolds; it's allowed to reign and command your next choice, becoming your natural authority and power. It's a give-and-take process for the student-warrior. As we recognize the way thoughts keep us from being centered in calm-concentration, we're more able to (gently) bring them under control and begin to trust the process.

Once you can sense or "hear" your intuition—the guiding action not based on fear or indecision—even once, and recognize it, you will want to hear it again. It comes through (consciously or not) as a clear, unemotional and unquestionable sound, voice, knowing, or deep feeling, that you will act upon with certainty, especially when the mind is free of circulating or restricted thoughts. You might notice times you have said or will remark, "I just knew I had to do this." This is the Great Shifting, the gradual exchange that occurs, when we allow ourselves to walk gently, think gently, act gently.

As you reach greater depths of quiet and peace through Concentrated-Awareness, you'll gain a foothold, a little leverage, that offers a view of what *can be*, and will want more of the self-freedom that it brings. As your intuition sharpens for the first time, you will begin to realize there is relief from the disquieted mind—there is relief from worry, doubt, chatter, disorder, and fear, and that *you can* actively bring your mind under rule through your will, and benefit greatly.

That is victory.

LESSON ONE (1–7): CHANGING YOUR HABITS

Since commands come naturally through the intuition, the more we root our conscious life in concentration, through attention, the more we'll be able to get hold of the treasure of pure-knowing. The more aware we are, the more we will engage circumstances from the *right way*[4] of thinking—we will see difficulty as opportunity, and opportunity as another moment to show up with a clear heart and mind.

We ultimately exchange what we deem a negative belief for a neutral sense of openness to all moments that come equally. And with the mind under a new rulership, we recognize our ability to *always* choose, through free will, how we experience the next moment, surrendering to the new freedom of a course without resistance.

Once we've experienced a mental state of equanimity, the Gentle-Way opens up and becomes more apparent. We recognize it was always with us; we become aware of what was hidden: all experiences are one long evolving or unfoldment, without a beginning or an end. We become limitless, able to conceive any dream or possibility, no longer restricted to common consciousness bound by thoughts/senses/emotions.

But be mindful.

Sun Tzu is offering us the path of experience, suggesting that we can miss the very deep-seated habits limiting our advancement. If you become aware of the patterns and repetitions, they will show you what you need to learn (to grow/evolve) and allow you to act accordingly.

An easy way to understand it is like this: we're always with our inner teacher, the Intuitive-Unfolding. Sometimes it gets our attention very quickly, like when we're not paying attention while driving and suddenly, a bird flies close to the windshield, jolting us out of our daydream, just in time to hit the brakes and avoid an accident.

---

4   "Right way," used here, is echoing the title of Sun Tzu's treatise, which is sometimes referred to as the "right way of war." The "right way" is perceived when the Hidden Path to Peace and Wholeness appears unadulterated; one recognizes that all actions are pure and one's purpose is to give ceaselessly in an ever-exchange that is in harmony with all things, a sensation that often is deemed "right" versus the mental enslavement of competition and resistance.

Other times, we can hear it, but just don't listen. We allow our limiting (habitual) ideas to get in the way. We do things all the time that we know aren't good for us and then say, "I knew I shouldn't have done that!" In hindsight, we can see how our intuition was there offering us a way around that obstacle.

In time, as we regulate our mind, bringing our consciousness to deep concentration, we hear our inner teacher and its truth more freely and often. We then cut down the amount of time from one obstruction to the next. Eventually, we no longer deliberate through thinking, but simply exist in a state of knowing when and where to act.

Gradually, we no longer experience challenges; we see a long line of infinite moments unfolding, and we're in flow with it.[5]

But to start, we very much separate work, family, play, spiritual matters, and so on, into different areas, and so too, separate the challenges from the opportunities. Because we're great at compartmentalizing the areas of our life, we will not readily see that the difficult boss, the almost-accident, the frustrating relationship, or the antagonistic experience at a checkout are generally impacting us in similar ways, creating a pattern or lesson from which to learn (occurring in a cycle).

At the same time, *what we learn* often has less to do with *outer* matters, but more to do with the *inner* shifting of a habit or limited way of thinking, which alters our perceptions (which in turn, can create boundless freedom and unity).

If we become attentive to the repetitious lessons and cycles, and make improvements/changes, our perception (of reality) will reorder and also change. In time, we will naturally spend less time focused outwardly, devoting more time to inward reflection, focused on the Inner Sun, the ultimate seat of rulership. (Eventually, we no longer experience a separation of an inner/outer world, but one that is Whole).

Sun Tzu is asking us to be *aware* of the mental patterns, the things you complain about over and again that are limiting you. Sun Tzu says, "It would be foolish to take them with you," meaning, you can't reach a mental state of harmony, if you are constantly in a limited state of distress over the same matters that distract your focus. And just when you think you have overcome a limiting trait (such as unworthiness, pettiness, jealousy, etc.),

---

5   An example of this can be found in Zoroastrianism. Verethragna is the representation of both the obstacle and the victory, or giver of victory, suggesting that through our ability to traverse the perception of obstacles, we succeed. In so many words, every moment is perfect and in harmony, and we rise to meet it with our very best love, care, and empathy.

there will be another... you might even be fooled into thinking you've made great change in your life, but there is still more hiding in the recesses of the mind (or field of perception) for you to discover. Each time you overcome one trait, you will gain a new foothold, and continue on the journey.

Be wise, recognize your patterns and repetitions, and change them.

LESSON TWO (8–13): PRACTICING A CALM MIND

Sun Tzu is demonstrating how the most powerful thoughts can constantly take us away from our seat of concentration. Each time we're pulled into a thought-thread, we'll grow fatigued, mentally, and deplete our vital energy, limiting our chances of unifying our mind. Remember, Wholeness isn't the outcome of a series of steps that you will achieve, but a state of Constant-Awareness existing *right now*—it is the power of restless thoughts that will keep the mind from perceiving with clear awareness that this state of mind is simultaneously occurring along with the distraction.

It happens the same way, when we perceive difficulty. If you're having a really good day but then something "bad" happens, the only thing that changed from one experience to the next is the shift in your perception—the mind that labeled the experience "bad." Through mastery of the mind, we begin to see we are in control of how we view an experience. Good/bad, difficulty/opportunity, they coexist. We often choose to see one over the other—the one that favors us, or the one that is habitually ingrained from our reactions or responses.

False ideas can be penetrated, observed, cut-off, surrounded—this is the core of Sun Tzu's teaching. The more we pay attention (Concentrated-Awareness), the more we see our repetitions, and the more likely, or possible, it is that we can make a change and "think" (as well as "be") in a different way.

Gradually, as we lessen the obstacles of restless or habituated thoughts, we are able to recognize how we've accepted a limited state of consciousness; so much so, that the duality of good/bad dissipates—we see that it is our choices making us suffer and opt for freedom instead. In time, we see all existence (or experiences) as simply occurring. Then when two events occur, like you wake up with a rash on your birthday, or you get laryngitis the same day you're supposed to give an important speech, you meet it with wonder and lightness, oneness and curiosity, knowing that the experience itself is a treasure.

However, to begin, we can become much more aware of how powerful our thoughts are in establishing how we think and live, or craft our version of reality, one often based on emotional responses. We can regain control, assert a new rulership, like Sun Tzu is advising, simply by starting with the ideas weighing most prominently that are causing us to lose our ambition and will.

In other words, *the thought most dominating your mind is in a war against your concentration.*

Luckily, Sun Tzu shows us that harmony is possible in each moment, when we recognize our truest nature. Gradually, we recognize the wandering attention we experience, without mental rest, is in our control. We can make up our mind to not be angry ever again; we can choose not to be afraid in favor of recognizing that fear exists only in our mind, nowhere else.

For example, you might happen to be at home with another person and you both hear a noise; one is scared, one is not. If you're the one who's scared, you can actively question the fear, and get on the other side of it to see it is not real—only your belief in it is. Likewise, if you are the one not experiencing fear, through empathy, you can understand the other person who *is* experiencing it.

Our perception of our circumstances will dictate our reactions, and essentially calculate the course of our next unfolding. Through concentration and attention, we will be able to choose a more direct course and action, aligned with our inner harmony. The sooner we can recognize that we're leaving our mental balance, the faster we can let go, allow, and resume it, rather than letting the mind wander and root deeper into confusion.

LESSON THREE (14–23): TUNING IN TO YOUR INTUITION

Our intuition is our greatest strength because it is not impacted by our emotions and senses. When we recognize our Intuitive-Unfolding, it's pure truth. As you uncover your hidden teacher, you will enjoy your company, your creativity, your love/joy, prompting you to cultivate a new awareness toward life that is unshakable.

When you act from your Inner Sun, you never doubt it, because you have an inward knowing that is not verbal. You get glimpses of this natural state and can evolve your experience to a point where it will be constant and you never leave it. When this happens, the mental conflicts go away; you will no longer be in a state of war with yourself. You recognize your intuition, your Inner Sun, as the sole Commander and guide, and will therefore see your usual conscious thoughts as false impressions attempting to unseat your wisdom/truth.

Since Intuitive-Unfolding is true-truth, you will see thoughts more like ghosts, falsely haunting your field of perception, and give them no power, allowing them to fade. And as your circumstances change, Sun Tzu is asking you to keep "dividing" the thoughts as they come, so that they can't grow strong and unseat you—they are and will be deceiving; it is easy to fall back into old patterns as you encounter old places, friends, and circumstances, so be mindful and prepared for these circumstances that will arise and test you.

Simply assert your will and quell the unruly thoughts or old habits, like an unmovable mountain. Remember, through concentration and attention attuned to your Intuitive-Unfolding, you can go into any situation and not be triggered or pulled from your inner source.[6] This is why you don't see a regulated practice time in Sun Tzu's work, since the battlefield exists in every circumstance and each moment—at the supermarket, on the highway, at work, on vacation, right before sleep, in the shower—all experiences are the same experience. You're never in a position where you can't regulate your mind in Concentrated-Awareness.

The idea, situation, or circumstance that presents itself, keeping you distracted, is your "battlefield." The only war being fought is the one you generate and perceive. Assert your "inner" will over your "outer" will, or establish conscious-unity, and you'll regain your seat of concentration and focus, giving you victory, even if it's temporary—thus, *your concentration will be like a thunderbolt.*

When a new thought-cycle begins, take the same action and disband and disperse the thoughts. Pay them no mind and your whole Self will benefit. You can actually ponder and deliberate what thoughts arise. As you clear them, more will come, including ideas you will wonder about. You may ask where they even came from, but there they are! It's like when you wake up with a song in your head and have no recollection of where you've even heard it.

As the mind cycles through thoughts, through observation, you can calculate the next moment, and assert concentration to act in conjunction with your intuition to achieve inner silence from external noises or involvement from the senses that might unseat your attention. Gradually, inner harmony prevails, as you regain a calm, natural state of equanimity. It's like finally having full control of the volume on the radio frequency for your conscious thoughts.

---

6   This idea is echoed in Psalm 23: "Lo, though I walk through the valley of the shadow of death, I will fear no evil," which suggests a mastered mind unimpeded by external forces that would try to break the concentrated focus of unification with God.

LESSON FOUR (24–37): LETTING THOUGHTS COME AND GO

Honoring the Gentle-Way, we can utilize the practice of routinely bringing our ears and eyes (all our senses) to a point of focus so that they don't disturb the mind. Solitude and quiet are superior methods to support mental harmony. But to begin, or as you navigate your day-to-day activities—or even as a meditation practice—you can keep the senses focused on something, which will help allow the intuition a clear channel of communication by minimizing thoughts.

If you walk and listen to music, the sound will keep your ears busy, while the walking will keep your conscious mind busy. Both, together, allow the intuition freedom to unfold, to gain strength and be heard. If you are a runner or practice any type of sport, gardening, martial arts, knitting, or puzzles, the action distracts the conscious mind, enabling your awareness to be still and gain clarity and peace. Equally, when we give the eyes something to look at, our focus goes there, rather than on following a thought, which will "rob" the mind of its gentle-calm.

Sun Tzu offers the concept of working with the mind at different times of the day, allowing us to make modifications to our daily activities. If we know the "mind's moods" ahead of time—say, we are usually more alert and focused in the morning, and by the evening may find ourselves sluggish—we can concentrate more during the weak times to keep our mental calm. Ultimately, if we retain our self-awareness by recognizing the situations that arise are challenging our resolve to remain disciplined and calm, we won't readily give the kingdom of our mind over to distraction and disorder.

We can evolve to a state of Peace and Wholeness—always present and available, but often hidden—by being aware, as the next thought arises, and allow it to pass with ease. We can weigh its importance, but not let it unseat our concentration and steal our vital energy or focus. This is how harmony and peace become our natural state. We anticipate moments where we might stumble—such as when we feel anger rising—and act accordingly to avoid losing our center.

Thoughts come and go effortlessly, so there is no need to be forceful or get frustrated if you can't "clear" them. The greatest action is effortless-allowing, which essentially gives no attention to our straying thoughts, thereby depriving them of strength. To allow thoughts to go freely is a step toward your own mental victory.

PRACTICING CALCULATED-AWARENESS

If you've ever asked someone for advice, you know what it's like to be uncertain. It seems common that we would seek the help of others to find our way forward, but what if you could know for certain what to do *all the time*—essentially to never live in doubt, fear, or worry—never to question a decision or wonder if you should've tried another way. Imagine what it would be like to have every moment unfold in harmony, without resistance or struggle.

Sun Tzu shows us that we can calculate the movement of our thoughts, to bring them under the Generalship of the concentration and attention, which in turn creates a climate of centered awareness. Everyone has experienced intuitive moments one time or another, perhaps a hunch, to go one way, rather than another. To suggest cultivating intuition almost seems too easy, but that's exactly what Sun Tzu is asking us to do. When we calculate with awareness our next thought, we begin to make room for our intuition to unfold and support our choices and decisions in a more natural way. Although our intuition is always available, you may not be attuned to it, instead ruled by the restless wandering mind, navigating still with uncertainty.

Sun Tzu is suggesting that if you discipline your mind through concentration and attention, you can turn off distractions long enough to hear and know your intuitive guidance. It is a knowing that is not thought with the mind, but is revealed as a felt-sense, possible through awareness.[7] Self-awareness is very clear, like an invisible angel prompting you with certainty to act, without doubt or confusion; it's like have a "gut feeling" and trusting it wholeheartedly.

As you regulate your mind, your focus becomes less fixated on the thought-tangents, so much so, you will, on occasion, notice you're not even thinking. It is a different way of navigating the world—for example, not hearing the chatter when you come and go from a store; or you travel a highway and don't need a radio, nor have your own mental radio blaring because you are free of thought.[8]

7   This lends once more to the words of Socrates: "What I know is that I know nothing." Plato is giving voice to the presence of Intuitive-Knowing, or one's intuitive consciousness, which can't be thought but is Whole and experienced as present awareness, guided by pure intuition.
8   The state of sleep can offer a reprieve from thoughts, and present the student with their first insight into the clear channel that lies within. But sleep can also be dictated by dreams that are packed with movie-like adventures and mishaps that further create a lack of peace and harmony, which is then carried over into (the perception of) waking.

Sun Tzu's advice is to be attentive to what thought might come in and break that field of concentration and calm. Through those moments, you're not thought-less, but rather allowing for the field of intuition to unfold without restricting it. This Intuitive-Unfolding is like an internal GPS system taking you into the certain future—it becomes certain, since you are in a state of wonder, curiosity, and indifference, because all situations arising can be met with gentle ease and care, love and harmony, unity and cooperation (versus an uncertain future dictated by fear, worry, doubt, and competition).

We can easily test out our intuition and observe that it's there acting on our behalf, then create a deeper relationship. There is never a time it is not present, so we can engage it now by listening, rather than reacting. It will take time for you to know the difference between your Intuitive-Knowing and just wishes or guesses. You might try to simply ask to be shown the way forward. If nothing presents, accept that you're exactly where you need to be, or that the answer will come as needed. Allow, rather than assert any thinking that will only bring endless words and thought-tangents. Inner awareness is much quieter and gentler. It acts without force and so will you.

Time is not the same when we allow our intuition to carve the Gentle-Way of our conscious life. It is suspended and ceases to exist. Whether something happens, or doesn't, will eventually be unimportant, as you will experience a sense of being in the moment, recognizing it is unfolding ceaselessly, along with your intuition.

Equally, you may sense cycles—you might recognize that many things are being moved to create scenarios and outcomes, and they are all beneficial to you. This is what unity feels like as intuition becomes your ally, essentially becoming your companion and teacher, your guide, the one that *is you* and also guides you.

Life becomes circular, as the mental wars that gained your focus yesterday no longer have the power to distract you. People, places, circumstances, difficulties, become opportunities to give of your gifts, especially love.

Calculated-Awareness comprises all the steps Sun Tzu has provided thus far. When you practice and master each step, you naturally evolve and become intuitively stronger. You can observe and calculate the mind in each unfolding moment, on the circular journey of the Gentle-Way, to unfold self-awareness. As you develop your concentration and attention, it will be like "the momentum of a round stone rolling down a mountain thousands of feet high," meaning, it gains strength.

Begin now to recognize your own cycles and patterns, to see moments and gaps in your thinking when intuition is the one guiding you. Deepen your attention and focus, so you no longer give up your freedom to unruly thoughts, but allow your inner wisdom to reveal itself. Pay attention to when your vital energy or will wanes, and what circumstances steal them most, and investigate why. Your emotions and senses will continuously create wars for you to fight; but through concentration and attention, you can regain your foothold of inward silence.

With a little practice, if you can forgo frustration, you will see how quiet and gentle you can become. So much so, you will not want to leave a trace of your restless mental energy/thought anywhere you go! Like the "Leave no trace behind" sign seen in parks or forests, advocating leaving only footprints (versus trash), you will become so focused that you won't even wish to leave a thought (energy) behind for someone else to sense.

You can regulate your mind to ensure you won't leave your mental "trash" or vibration *anywhere* you go, while actively elevating others (consciously or not) through your natural state of joy and love.

This is where our social responsibility to serve others takes on a more valued meaning and experience: we recognize we have a lot to offer the world. Every step is another moment to share and serve on the Gentle-Way.

As your natural state is restored to balance, you will emit a new vibration; others will (consciously or not) feel it and grow lighter. Your presence alone can stop a verbal war or disagreement, which is only the beginning of your influence!

You will naturally feel your inward joy seeping into all areas of your life, until you recognize it as one, unified Whole. If a mental battle arises, you will apply the strategy you took and regain the kingdom.

Be gentle with yourself and you will be victorious.

THE SEVENTH STEP ON THE HIDDEN PATH TO PEACE AND WHOLENESS

1. Apply the Hidden Path to Peace and Wholeness in whatever way best reveals itself to you in order to establish Calculated-Awareness right now.

2. Recognize opportunities, moment to moment, to maintain a presence of Calculated-Awareness, allowing restless thoughts to fade and disappear, freeing your intuition to "speak" or "be heard" clearly.

3. Notice intuitive moments throughout the day. For example, if you are expecting a loved one home, see if you can intuit the exact time; if you are waiting on news, intuit when the news will arrive and even how. Attune to it, filtering out the negative/habituated conscious chatter that normally hinders you.

Calculated-Awareness Practice is the seventh step on the Hidden Path to Peace and Wholeness. Never give up or tire in your effort to establish deeper awareness in all that you do. The more you direct, calculate, and bring your mind toward a state of awareness, the more your intuition will shine forth, making your life more certain and harmonious.

Ruminations: Calculated-Awareness Practice

"A mind without concentration is lost."

– Chapter 7

- -

1. Share a time when you were aware of your intuition. What are some of the ways that you know you are "hearing" or "sensing" your intuition, as opposed to just hearing your conscious mind?

- -

2. Share a time when you experienced deep concentration and attention on a particular project. What are some of the characteristics you experienced when being very deeply focused or aware?

- -

3. Intuitive-Unfolding suggests that our intuition is ever-present, unfolding in each moment. Looking back at the last day or week, can you see a particular thread of experiences that were essentially guided by your intuition?

- -

4. Take a situation where you heard your intuition but didn't follow it. What were the factors in that situation that were stronger, misleading you?

- -

5. On the Hidden Path to Peace and Wholeness, what are some strategies you can create to help you let go of the "all-ruling" war in your mind and just allow your thoughts to pass?

6. Take a difficult situation that happened in the last day, week, or month, and rewrite it in a way that turns difficulty into opportunity, misfortune into gain, deviousness into honesty.

7. Name three deep-seated thinking habits that might be fooling you into creating cyclical patterns. How might you get them under control and establish a new course?

8. Share a time when you had a very strong habit/emotion at the forefront of your mind that wouldn't let you go. How long did the thought-thread last? Were you fatigued and anxious? How did it eventually get resolved? (If it hasn't, what can you apply from Sun Tzu's teaching to regain deeper concentration?)

9. Share a time when you actively pondered and deliberated on the thoughts coming/going in your field of consciousness and were able to not be moved by or follow them. (Try this now if you need to).

10. Choose something you think about often (or fixate on) and investigate it. Spend time noticing when you think about this topic, then make up your mind to regulate it. For example, if you're quick to anger, make up your mind not to allow it to unseat your concentration. Simply return to your center of calm and try again.

11. What time of the day do you find you have the least focus and ability to concentrate? What strategies can you incorporate daily to maintain your gentle-center?

12. Write about a time that your mind baited or tempted you to surrender your calm. What can you do next time to avoid the temptation?

8

VARIATIONS OF METHOD

1. Sun Tzu said: when observing the mind, the student receives their commands from the Intuitive-Unfolding managing the senses and concentrating their will.

2. When the mind is difficult to settle, don't let your attention remain. When the mind is in hostile territory, enlist the aid of calmness. Do not let the mind linger on ideas/thoughts that will keep you dangerously from your concentrated center. In severe cases, you must resort to undertaking a stratagem. In desperate situations, you must fight to get your mind free of the entanglement.

3. There are strong thoughts that *must not be followed*; emotions that *must not be challenged*; senses that *must not be allowed to overwhelm*; situations that *must not be confronted*; commands of the restless, disquieted mind *that must not be obeyed*. These are the Five Advantages.

4. The student-warrior who thoroughly understands the advantages that accompany the variations of method—or knowledge of the Five Advantages—knows how to handle the restless mind.

5. The student who does not understand these may be well acquainted with the nature (or disposition) of the mind—and the way they habitually think—yet they will not be able to use this knowledge to any advantage.

6. So the student observing (the mind), who is unversed in the art of varying their method, even though they are acquainted with the Five Advantages, will fail to make the best use of their self-control/self-possession.

7. Whether in an advantageous or disadvantageous mental state, the wise student-warrior will aim for a harmonious state of consciousness.

8. If our aspiration of harmony is strengthened in this way, we may establish the vital component of our (chosen) planned method.

9. If, on the other hand, in the midst of mental difficulties we are always ready to regain our will (composure), to gain the advantage and restore harmony, we may alleviate any further adversity.

10. Reduce the hostile thought-threads by intentionally disrupting them from continuing, and deliberately keep them flowing, so as to not to let them burrow and multiply. Recognize that what may seem true is really misleading and false, luring you to perceive the thoughts as all-powerful, when really, you can disband and disperse them.

11. The gentle art of observing the mind teaches us to rely not on the likelihood of the thoughts *not* coming, but on our own readiness to *receive them*; and not on the chance of them attacking, but on the fact we have first made our concentration impenetrable.

12. There are Five Potential Limitations that may affect the student's equanimity:

    a.   Recklessness, which leads to shattered concentration.
    b.   Cowardice, which leads to being overtaken by habituated limitations.
    c.   A hasty temper, which can be provoked easily by criticism.
    d.   A sensitive nature, which leads easily to feeling shame or humiliation.
    e.   An overly anxious emotional state, which exposes them to worry and difficulty.

13. These are the five persistent shortcomings of the student, which are ruinous to the discipline of observation.

14. When the Intuitive-Unfolding is unheard, and the student's concentration is stolen, the cause will surely be found among these Five Potential Limitations. Let them be a subject of rumination.

INTERPRETING THE LIVING WISDOM OF SUN TZU

Sun Tzu explains how the mind will strategically work against you, to defeat your efforts, and offers the student-warrior the strategy of *variations of method* to continue gaining footholds toward victory (over surrender) for a balanced, harmonious mind.

If you have been practicing the preceding steps on the Hidden Path to Peace and Wholeness, you might already be experiencing improvements. The more you clear your field of perception (e.g., allowing thoughts to pass without restriction; overcoming perceived limitations, etc.), the more old patterns, ideas, beliefs, and so forth, will shake free, but also may turn up again to steal your focus. It will seem like you uproot one obstacle and then there are three more, and three more after that.

As the field of perception goes through cycles, and roots out distractions, it will not surrender easily, and keep throwing more at you, knowing what will defeat you easily. And it's not just your mind, but also your body and environment that act as willful opponents.

To help, Sun Tzu offers us the Five Advantages for observing the mind:

1. Strong thoughts must not be followed.
2. Strong emotions must not be challenged.
3. Strong senses must not be allowed to overwhelm.
4. Tenacious situations must not be confronted.
5. Demands from the restless mind must not be obeyed.

The goal is to know each advantage so well that you can recognize when they are happening to you and then take action.

Once we have developed our concentration through attention, we can gain a foothold of understanding that our thoughts are not permanent, and can come and go, without our interference. By employing the strategy of the Five Advantages, we can observe each thought and recognize how it might lead to an emotion, or engage our senses; we can anticipate how our conscious mind can be easily moved to act, believing it has come up with the best course. But it's often a tangled course, a false one, not necessarily derived from inner silence, which gives freedom to our intuition. The more we cut off the flow of thought and energy to our emotions/senses, the deeper our concentration, the more we can calculate our best course. Going foward, our decisions and choices, our future, will become more focused and in accord with our highest purpose.

LESSON ONE (1–10): WAYS TO RESIST THOUGHTS

Besides utilizing the Five Advantages to observe the mind, Sun Tzu is providing more reconnaissance for dealing with the "enemy" of the mind. When we experience moments that unsettle the mind, it sprouts with thoughts fueled by emotions, so we can enlist our weapon of calmness to deliberately refocus our attention and not linger on the thoughts trying to rule us.

In severe cases, we might have to invoke a strategy to gain leverage, like making light of the situation, redirecting our attention, or interrupting ourselves mid-thought. This is where Sun Tzu reminds us this is a battle—or at least that it might feel like one—and we have to "fight," which in this case can be done through our awareness of the Five Advantages.

As we quiet the mind, through deeper concentration and attention, we must vary our technique—this is because the mind will, even close to harmony, cleave to another pattern. Since the disquieted mind can lead us away from balance and harmony, we're warned that just knowing the strategies isn't enough; we can still lose the advantage.

In the same way you wouldn't go toward the goal and execute the same moves against an opponent in hockey or soccer because your opponent can anticipate your actions, so too, the body and the mind can anticipate what you will do. If you can get leverage through direct observation, interrupting the flow of thoughts, and alter your usual method by redirecting your focus, you might just gain the advantage and regain your seat of concentration.

Always aim to harmonize your thoughts/actions, etc. and reassert your will—that's very important. We can reestablish our volition and demand a new course/outcome to whatever we're facing. We can choose not to be angry; we can choose to remain harmonious. We can elect to see our thoughts as misleading and untrue, and be free of the limitations and beliefs they might impose. This is how we create a new state of equanimity as a way of life. We eliminate adversity just by asserting our Concentrated-Awareness over our emotions and senses. Apply concentration and attention by centering awareness and regain your inner kingdom of silence.

At the least, when you find yourself in a "hostile" stronghold of thoughts, deliberately disrupt, disperse, and recognize them as falsely leading you astray to end the skirmish.

LESSON TWO (10–14): FACING SHORTCOMINGS

Sun Tzu is asking you to face yourself, just as you would an invading army on the battlefield, and to also recognize the Five Potential Limitations, in order to gain an advantage. This is the type of self-work taught in the

Inner Sun schools in Sun Tzu's day, allowing each student the wisdom to see the shortcomings of their mind and to offer a gentle way of evolving, in order to restore peace.

Since it's probable that the army of thoughts will continue to invade, we need to vary our method, when the next thought arises, in order to clear the battlefield (so to speak). Then we can become attuned to the Wholeness of all life, and rather than feel separate (or singular), we experience expansion as being part of a whole, and our consciousness is allowed an unobstructed view of our true nature.

Our readiness allows us to be in a state of awareness to act so our concentration cannot be penetrated. As Sun Tzu explains, the five short-comings that will arise are recklessness, cowardice, a hasty temper, a sensitive nature, and an overly anxious emotional state. We can have a strong predisposition toward one, or maybe we're experiencing all of them at the same time. Or perhaps we move from one shortcoming to the next. All of them do the same thing: they silence the intuition, our source, our clear and unbiased wisdom, which is essential to living whole lives.

On Sun Tzu's Hidden Path to Peace and Wholeness, it's important to know the Five Potential Limitations, and identify when and how they work. The more we investigate them and be truthful when we are acting out a shortcoming, the more we can anticipate what we will do in the next situation or circumstances and apply a variation of method or new strategy to gain a foothold.

VARYING STRATEGIES FOR A HARMONIOUS MIND

Our mind can be very elusive, or so we believe, especially when we start to observe it. The good news is that even our small efforts can make strong inroads into deeper concentration and harmony as a way of life. In fact, as soon as we begin to employ Sun Tzu's strategies and wisdom, we will notice it's like a game we are playing with ourselves.

When we win, so to speak—when we've *not* let our mind think carelessly or react to a situation habitually—we will like the results; we will want more of it. Then when we see more gains—say, your intuition is suddenly sharp and you notice each day you are getting insights and clues to the future through premonitions—you will realize it's because you have been attentive and mindful to abide in your hidden Peace and Wholeness.

Likewise, it can also go the other way.

You might be practicing and feel like you're making an effort with the strategies and POW! you get sideswiped into one (perceived) aggravating experience after another. And then it can feel like failure. But remember Sun Tzu's words: if you do the work in earnest, you're never starting over; and what feels like losing is actually helping you to break your resistance to change.

Difficulty is the opportunity to try again.

We may encounter different people or events or circumstances or details, but we're very much the same seasoned actor on the stage engaging our rehearsed lines and actions and creating yet another impressive performance. So be gentle with yourself and regard all situations as more practice to observe your responses and act anew.

We're ultimately being called to stop acting like we always do—to stop thinking the way we always do. It's really easy to hear ourselves repeat and respond. The neighbor's dog is barking again—and on cue, you remark about your irritation. It seems harmless, but what would happen if you varied the method of response, so you were not ruled by this experience pulling you out of your calm-balance, stirring your emotions?

If you have a family member who knows exactly how to get you to rise to anger, rather than respond or anticipate *their* actions, you can *anticipate your own* by utilizing the Path to Peace and Wholeness. What if you were to *not* act like you always do? (That's self-responsibility, the act of recognizing your own part in every circumstance). Usually, we put the emphasis and blame on others, like the difficult parent, employer, stranger, and so on. We typically blame others, yet rarely review our own mind and its participation and beliefs, which can solidify our way of thinking, preventing change.

Even if the "terrible" thing done to us by another is real and acknowledged, we may lock the other person into a (mental) prison that doesn't allow them to ever be anyone else. As we're typically bound by habits, we rarely ever observe our own part, actions, and method of response, no matter the conflict. If both parties remain intransigent and unchanged, then there is never a truce, only ever a battle. According to Sun Tzu, we can vary our predictable nature and free ourselves. We can stop our tangents, our beliefs, and let them go.

When we show up to see the harmful coworker/boss or parent and vary how we act/think, they too will have to interrupt the way they are thinking about us. In fact, if you vary your thoughts/actions, it gives others the chance to change too. And even if they don't, it's okay, because you are changing. Your energy shifts the situation and the stronghold it has in your mind to one of harmony. But you have to take responsibility for your thoughts and beliefs that are very deeply rooted. You can let them go at any time. This is the act of effortless-allowing and not carrying the thought further.

What we can't see (before letting go) is how our thoughts fashion *all* our relationships and events/circumstances, and that by varying our thoughts with new ones, or none at all, we change the course of our future, and sometimes even the past (see Varying Your Method exercise), and can establish a deeper concentration and harmony.

If, for example, you and your spouse argue over a particular thing, you may wait for it to happen, just to dig in and lose your harmony. But if you don't engage, failing to provide your typical response, they will have no recourse, nor will they have an acting partner, and be forced to come up with a new line. Since your thoughts can't multiply, the situation can become like new, and you can rewrite a future where you never act out this scenario again.

In the process, you can begin to address all areas of your life with a new weapon—the ability to vary your actions and responses to everything *every-where*—and it's actually a lot of fun! You can even plan a whole day of doing and thinking in opposite or new or extraordinary ways. The day will be filled with surprises, especially from the people who take comfort in having things remain the same. They will expect the same you, who thinks and tends to say the same thing over and over too, but you'll show them a new version of you!

As you vary your responses, watch how prone you are to one of the five shortcomings (recklessness, cowardice, a hasty temper, a sensitive nature, and an overly anxious emotional state). You can start with one of them, and all day, think and do differently.

Another way to *vary your method* is to offer healing and love to the things that arise. Be gentle with yourself and others, so that as a conflict emerges, you don't judge it, get rid of it, or get swept up by it.

When you notice a thought that is aggravating or distracting your senses/emotions, you can interrupt it and investigate it, discovering why you have it, why it returned, and see it truthfully, rather than succumb to the impression that has rooted itself like a photograph in your memory and may or may not be true, or even have power over you anymore.

EXERCISE:
VARY YOUR METHOD TO HEAL THE PAST

Try the following exercise to help you vary your method and heal the past:

First, think of a relationship past or present where the other person caused you difficulty, hurt, or even harm. As you begin, your mind will carry you over the images in memory, like an army traveling over the valleys and streams of events, supported by the emotions you experienced. Once you have seen the experience or event from your side, reverse it and see it from *their* side.

As you visit their version of the story, consider who they were and how they may have ended up at that place, same time as you. Embody compassion and empathy not only for yourself, but for the other person, in order to see different qualities they possess that you may not have ever considered, or are opposite of the way you have always felt or believed about them.

Consider how your own thoughts have molded, shaped, and made firm the person and the event, making it so it's unchanged and permanent, despite how much you and the other person have evolved since then. Take note of these changes.

Without any physical action, you can create a new story and memory that varies from the fixed past to incorporate these newly discovered changes, which will essentially heal the past (or present) that you've memorized by offering yourself a new way forward through love and forgiveness. In doing so, you can free yourself and the other person (and anyone else involved) of the emotion and thought that has been held frozen in time.

As an example, you might mentally say, *I accept responsibility for the way I perceive and think about this event and/or person. I accept love; I receive love. I accept forgiveness: I receive forgiveness. I will no longer live bound to the emotions felt, instead I wash it with peace and compassion.* Likewise, you can also mentally affirm, *I offer/give love to this event/person; I offer/give forgiveness, that we may both be healed of the emotions and thoughts felt. May this moment be washed with peace, compassion, and love. I forgive them; may they forgive me. I offer love; may they see me with love too.*

The more you vary your usual way of thinking about any given moment, the more you can see that your emotions—their power to rule your thoughts or memory—are often frozen and incongruent. We essentially create monuments to hurtful events and can essentially take them down and free the other person, in the process. When we do, we free our own energy, our own frailty and innocence, our bitterness, and exchange it for love.

This is the power of observation: to see and not do, or think the same thing over and again. We can call up the image of a person or a moment and pass judgment, true or untrue. In our mind, we're tying it to emotion, which in turn, shapes it as an unchanging concrete presence, like a ghost that then dictates our life through this sentiment or belief. Awareness can grant us a space to peel back a layer of perception, to see the world as changing and in flow and set a new course.

Over time, as thoughts arise, repeat this recipe of release (over being triggered to reestablish the event as a form again), taking into account the physical place it occurred, bystanders, witnesses, etc., who might've been impacted, sending love and forgiveness to all and then also receive it. The more you change your thoughts, the more freedom will come, until the thought-thread will disintegrate in your field of perception.

Unexpectedly, you may find months later that the individuals involved may show up in your reality again, slightly changed and new, because of the shift of energy. Thought fields aren't isolated, so when you take action to release the hurt, the emotions, etc., in one place, you free it everywhere. This is how Wholeness is achieved.

We have to be willing to really observe what we are thinking and how we remember, and cultivate our thoughts to the point that they seem set in concrete. When you change, you also allow others to change too. When we see only hurt, we experience only hurt; when we offer love, love is returned in our field of perception.

Vary the way you routinely think/act, and you will be victorious in reshaping the past, as well as the present, and actively create a new future. In time, you will only experience the effortless, unfolding moment, guided by intuition, which will never steer you wrong.

THE EIGHTH STEP ON THE HIDDEN PATH TO PEACE AND WHOLENESS

1. Apply the Hidden Path to Peace and Wholeness in whatever way best reveals itself to you in order to establish varying strategies right now.

2. Recognize opportunities, moment to moment, to vary the way you routinely act—be unpredictable; do something a different way; free yourself from old patterns, memories, hurts, shames, and experiences that are keeping you from inner harmony. Observe your mind and know it.

3. Notice moments throughout the day when you are acting out of habit or based on past judgments. Pick a person or situation that brings difficulty and observe your thoughts. (Journal them if this helps). Investigate and free yourself. Be willing to heal your past and your present responses. Be mindful of your own shortcomings to overcome them.

Variations of Method is the eighth step on the Hidden Path to Peace and Wholeness. The more you can know the Five Advantages and Five Shortcomings, the more likely you will begin to create new thoughts and outcomes for your life.

Observe and address your mental thought patterns.

Be willing to let go and apply the Gentle-Way of observation, to not be overwrought by your emotions and senses.

Let inner harmony be your compass in all matters.

Ruminations: Variations of Method

"The student who thoroughly understands the advantages that accompany the variations of method knows how to handle the restless mind."

– Chapter 8

----

1. Detail a situation when your thoughts swept you up in emotion and you were unable to get your mind under control. In hindsight, what method could you have employed to regain control?

----

2. Share a time when you allowed a strong emotion to get out of control and how you might now, or in the future, maintain your inner harmony.

----

3. Share a time when you allowed your senses to go unchecked and how you might now, or in the future, maintain your inner harmony.

----

4. Share a situation that got out of hand—or where you knew you should not have acted, but did anyway. What were the results of your actions? How could you now, or in the future, remain centered?

5. List some recent moments when you listened to the demands of your restless mind and did not like the outcome. What can you do now, or in the future, to win back the territory of the mind and assert your will, so as to avoid the same outcome?

6. Of the five shortcomings, which one are you most prone to and why?

7. What strategies can you employ if you have a disposition toward one of the five shortcomings?

8. Of the five shortcomings, which one do you feel gives you the least amount of concern and why?

9. Based on your answer to number 4, are there any strategies you are aware of that make you less prone to this shortcoming? How did you overcome it or avoid letting it rule you?

10. How important is intuition when facing the Five Shortcomings or Five Advantages?

11. In what way can you vary your method of response to achieve a new outcome? For example, if you have the same argument with someone, how can you take responsibility for your part in it, and create a new outcome?

12. Attune to your intuition on a problem going on in your mind today and write down what you believe is the intuitive way forward. Spend time asking for and attuning to the answers, and then measure the results and outcome. Be mindful of your conscious mind trying to trick you.

9

CONTEMPLATIVE-AWARENESS EXPANSION

1. Sun Tzu said: we come now to the question of expanding Contemplative-Awareness and observing signs of mental disturbances. Pass quickly over heightened troubles and keep in the neighborhood of expanding awareness that will continue to nourish you.

2. Attune your awareness in the highest (conscious) regions toward your Inner Sun (the sun's eye).[1,2] Such is the undertaking of *attuning awareness*.

3. After crossing over the river-threshold[3] of senses, you should not allow your concentration to be drawn back.

4. When an invading thought (or other sensation) crosses the sense-threshold, do not let your attention "advance" to meet it and lose your centered focus. It will be best to allocate a portion of Contemplative-Awareness to expand and then manage the disturbance.

5. If you are anxious to maintain your awareness, you should not go toward (or follow) the invading thought (or other sensation) near the sense-

---

1   The Inner Sun, or "sun's eye," has many names across cultures, like the Celtic *Sulis*, the Egyptian *Eye of Horus*, or the ancient Greek *Cyclops*, etc. Here in Sun Tzu's treatise, the Inner Sun is drawing your attention to the bright light and inner joy "seen" in expansive awareness.

2   Note: This illumination can occur with the eyes opened or closed. One's attention can always be centered here, at the sun's eye, as a point of observation through any activity.

3   The word "river" is used by Sun Tzu to indicate the rushing sound indicative of a flowing river that is often heard as the Observer (figuratively) crosses ordinary consciousness. All across time and cultures, sacred rivers have been used to symbolically depict this "crossing" over the (inner) threshold of consciousness (for example, the Ganga, Huang Ho, Nile, etc.).

threshold where it will arise, so that you can remain in Contemplative-Awareness.

6. Anchor your awareness "higher" than the sense-threshold, and attune to your Inner Sun. Do not "reverse" your awareness "back" toward the world of senses. Such is the undertaking of *anchoring awareness*.

7. If a confluence of difficult perceptions[4] is generated, your sole concern should be to surmount them quickly, without delay.

8. If forced to engage difficult perceptions (for example, your awareness wanders), you should gently relax into a state of effortless-allowing, rooted in nourishing joy. Such is undertaking of *relaxing awareness*.

9. When the mind is rooted in Contemplative-Awareness, it is like a dry, level county, where the thought-leaves have withered up. Take a calculated position in the rising ground (higher level of awareness) giving you the advantage of an unobstructed (clear) view of any new arising thoughts, thus creating a refuge. Such is the undertaking of *unrestricted awareness*.

10. These are the four beneficial insights of observation on the Gentle-Way, which empowers Contemplative-Awareness to vanquish the Four Distinct Animations (emperors).[5]

11. Contemplative-Awareness favors the higher realms of consciousness, centered on the ever-expanding Inner Sun over "returning" to the darkness (confusion) of the material world.

12. If you are careful with your perceptions and anchor your attention firmly, awareness will be free of the illusory suffering experienced by the body, and this will spell victory.

---

4   The word *perceptions* is used here as a broad term for "phenomena" that will appear in the field of deeper Contemplative-Awareness.

5   The Four Distinct Animations are what makes the body and material world appear fixed, solid, and enduring. They comprise: *that which is able to withstand wear* (solidity); *that which is able to unite* (cohesion); *that which is caused to move* (motion); and *that which is caused to change* (transmutation). Through the art of observation, the Observer grows aware of the distinct composites that interdependently create the material world (of form), thereby freeing the perception to recognize that what was thought to be solid changes and is in motion.

13. When you come to an obstruction, in the same way an army comes to a hill or an embankment, settle your attention on the Inner Sun, releasing any subjective reactions the mind is prone to. Thus, you will at once act for the benefit of your senses and utilize the natural advantages of the mind.

14. When ever-expanding Contemplative-Awareness faces obstructions that keep you from advancing (free of the body/material world) to the next expansion of consciousness, you must wait until the obstruction passes (through effortless-allowing).

15. Ever-expansive Contemplative-Awareness will experience the Five Interruptions arising to keep you attached to the body/material world. They are:

a. Interruptions from the physical body, which are like traversing *precipitous cliffs with torrents running between.*
b. Interruption from sensations/feelings that arise, which steal attention like *deep natural clouds passing by.*
c. Interruptions from thoughts and ideas, which act to keep you stuck *in confined places.*
d. Interruptions from shifting perceptions, which act like *tangled thickets to trap you.*
e. Interruptions from conscious attention of the Five Interruptions,[6] like mentally succumbing to *quagmires and crevices.*

The Observer should withdraw attention with speed and not engage with such circumstances when they arise.

16. While we keep away from such emotional interruptions, we can regulate our senses by "facing them"—allowing them to arise then fall away. This will "protect" our expanding awareness from having to retreat.

17. If protecting your ever-expanding awareness, be mindful to uproot those influences that will act like cunning spies to steal your concentrated-focus, and will attempt to "ambush" you to prevent you attaining the gentle-joy of the Inner Sun.

---

6   The Five Interruptions are "that which keeps the Observer rooted in material existence." Through observation, we can recognize that we are made up of changing atoms/matter, and thus break the "ego" or our perception's hold to expand our Contemplative-Awareness toward the Inner Sun of Wholeness and everlasting joy.

18. Emotional interruptions may seem subdued or quiet, but are often close at hand, naturally generating in the fields of consciousness. They can easily gain strength and then possession of one's established awareness.

19. When interruptions seem aloof (or distant) and try to provoke resistance, it is because they anticipate that the Contemplative-Awareness will mature and expand fully (leaving behind the causal world).

20. If emotional interruptions are given access to or consideration in the mind, it is baiting the Observer.

21. The Observer should be distrusting (suspicious) when the misty sense-objects appear on the outlying boundaries of consciousness, preparing to disturb their focus.

22. In the same way a scout would recognize the rising of birds in their flight as the sign of an ambush, so the Observer will know that a sudden "attack" is coming and Contemplative-Awareness may easily be broken.

23. When the mind is obstructed, it will continue to have faith in (cling to) the material world, causing more obstructions to appear, each one greater than the last. Like an army that advances first with chariots[7] then with infantry, the emotional interruptions will soon get a foothold, stifling the ever-expanding awareness.

24. When an emotional interruption is enticing, know that it is ready to advance and break your concentration. Likewise, if the interruption is desperate for your attention, it will soon retreat, if you have not believed in its ability to distract you.

25. When your Contemplative-Awareness loses accord with the Inner Sun, it is because the mental influences have come like chariots and taken up a position on the fringes of consciousness, urging you to engage.

---

7   Sun Tzu is comparing the mind—and its wandering thoughts and senses—to a chariot, which can "drag" your self-established awareness and presence away, hurriedly and with force. Heraclitus offered the same symbolism in The Logos, whereas Parmenides rides a chariot "into the house of Being," or inner consciousness, and is mentioned here to corroborate an understanding in the reader that Sun Tzu's treatise was a well-embraced body of knowledge over vast centuries, cultures, and traditions.

26. For calmness to prevail, it must be settled; if not, it can be usurped by the Five Interruptions.

27. When your attention roams, it is like soldiers falling into rank, and the critical moment will come to disturb your focus.

28. Be mindful to center your attention: hindrances that seem to come and go can be a lure to fully gain your attention.

29. *Dullness*—or a lack of interest—can develop and activate the body-senses.

30. *Agitation*—the inability to control without controlling—can cause distress and trigger the body-senses to respond.

31. If the disturbing perceptions have an advantage to pull you from the Inexhaustible[8]—it is that you've allowed them to exhaust your vital energy and willful effort.

32. Emptiness arises where interruptions are absent; fear, initiated by the senses, will shatter this state.

33. If there is interruption in expanding the Contemplative-Awareness, the Observer's authority—its rule—is weak. If the object of attention (centering on the Inner Sun) has shifted, the body/senses will revolt. If you get upset at the results, it is because your volition is weary.

34. When the Five Interruptions are at their strongest, they will figuratively *fight to the death* to shatter your expanding Contemplative-Awareness.

35. If you cater to complaints of the body/senses, you've lost your discipline, balance, and order.

36. The more you balance the mind with harmony, the more the disruptions will settle; restrict or try to control them and they will only take root more.

---

8   The *Inexhaustible* suggest the limitless, eternal All. There is no end to Wholeness found through the Inner Sun.

37. Using aggressive discipline and force to "get back" your balance shows a lack of intelligence.

38. When the outer interruptions are allowed to return to their natural stillness (resistance is withdrawn) balance is restored, the same way two opposing sides reach a mutual truce.

39. If the interruptions return full force—that which is sensed right in front of you—it demands great vigilance and attention.

40. If your awareness is vibrant and evenly matched to the arising objects, it cannot be overtaken (disrupted). What you can do is simply concentrate all your vital energy (your mental focus) to observe the arising interruptions and reinforce your will.

41. If the Observer doesn't exercise forethought, underestimating the power of the Five Interruptions, their attention will be taken over, breached.

42. Should you reprimand/restrict your awareness, it will not prove effective (for your awareness) to submit. If reestablishing discipline over the senses is not enforced, they will be useless in regaining concentration.

43. Therefore, your ability to contemplate and expand your awareness should be treated with gentle discipline to achieve certain victory.

44. If in training your awareness, you habitually reinforce gentle disciplines, you are more likely to succeed in your efforts; if not, you will experience failure.

45. If the Observer shows confidence in engaging the Contemplative-Awareness and insists on gentle-discipline, causing the interruptions to settle, the gain will be reciprocal.

INTERPRETING THE LIVING WISDOM OF SUN TZU

Until now, Sun Tzu has been training the student to work on strengthening their Contemplative-Awareness through the direct experience of observing the mind moment to moment. We need not go anywhere special to do that, but can be attentive to how we engage our daily life, *right now*: what we think; how we act; what we repeat or habituate as responses and reactions; what we fear and worry about; how joy is cultivated; what our relationships are to others; and so on. The more we contemplate awareness, and bring our attention and focus into balance and harmony, the stronger our connection to our Inner Sun will be.

As we grow, our concentration expands past the narrow focus of the little Self (or our daily conscious thoughts), and gains momentum toward the higher states of consciousness available to us all, and will (figuratively) peel back our perceptions of the material world. The more we settle our restless-ness, caused by distraction/distrubances, the deeper we can contemplate our essential nature (through the expansion of consciousness or oneness with our Inner Sun). At the same time, we develop a deeper awareness of the essence of reality, which we realize is ever-changing and in motion (e.g., matter, atoms, particles), and not fixed, but effortlessly flowing.

The more we grow aware of the Four Distinct Animations,[9] the more we perceive the natural, fluxing change of existence, the more we will recognize our interdependence to the "All," or Inexhaustible, or rather *Wholeness*. What makes all phenomena appear fixed, solid, and enduring can actually be experienced through the Four Distinct Animations as our own animated existence. We see "life" as composites that are essentially interdependently creating the causal world of form, thereby freeing the perception to recognize what we thought was solid is actually in motion, *changing*.

Our relationships and mindsets transform from regarding ourselves as living at the *center* of the wheel, to a more inclusive reciprocal relationship of perceiving the *whole* wheel, always in motion, evolving in perfect harmony. We recognize our uniqueness, while at the same time, our sameness and relationship to the Whole, and wonder, with concentrated attention, at the beautiful marvel unfolding, effortlessly, to which we are unfolding with too. Even constraints like time (for example, a burdened past or a worrisome future) and distance seem to disappear; even our thoughts

---

9   In other traditions they are also called the four elements or directions (five in different traditions); or four winds, the *Tatuye Topa*; or the four quarters of the Earth; or the Four Goddesses, Vijayä, Sujya, Ajita and Aparajita, who are undefeatable, always victorious (*Jayavaha*).

seem uncontained, but expand ... and can keep going, so long as we're not disturbed by anything.

Thus, Sun Tzu's elaborate advice shows us precisely what to expect when we observe our thoughts, as well as how to adopt strategies to "suffer" the least amount of (perceived) loss/failure and having the foreknowledge of what it might be like for you when you find yourself navigating expanded awareness. It's a detailed tour guide for the *country of the mind* (or the *field of perception*), with the highlights of experiences you can expect, places to avoid, best practices, and most of all, the costs involved if you end up off the beaten path.

LESSON ONE (1–10): FOUR TACTICS FOR CENTERING THE MIND
Sun Tzu doesn't waste any time explaining that the more you observe and contemplate your own mind (and existence), the more there is to distract and disturb you. When it's advised to "go quick" over mental interruptions, it's to show you that those interruptions arising can have no power over you if you allow them to pass without restriction—don't stop to regard your thoughts!

To help you find the truth yourself, Sun Tzu provides four tactics: *elevating*, *anchoring*, *relaxing*, and *unrestricting* your Contemplative-Awareness to be centered on your Inner Sun. With or without our eyes open, we bring our wandering mind to a masterful center-point on the "sun's eye." The more we do, the more our inner light permeates the facets of our perception.

These four methods sharpen our observation of the world, empowering us to "see" or perceive clearer; our awareness strengthens and the Gentle-Way opens, granting us the ability to recognize the Four Distinct Animations that essentially make our world appear solid.

In short, by recognizing their true nature—contemplating it, observing it—you will see your body is not the firm identity you perceive, but a changing composite just like all of existence. Why that's important is that an understanding comes that all existence is created by will and action: our will generates a thought that is directed and made into form. Having this knowledge, you then are no longer a limited body, but an unlimited creating will.

LESSON TWO (11–30): OVERCOMING OBSTRUCTIONS
Our Inner Sun truly wants freedom and will draw the conscious mind closer toward that beautiful inner light, which isn't separate but whole and in reciprocal relationship with all things. Keeping us from partaking in this joy or harmony, all the time, are the Four Distinct Animations,

which through our perception, moor our consciousness in the material body/world. As we deepen awareness, obstructions will arise, signaling our "descent" or return to ordinary reality. Through effortless-allowing (unrestricting our focus), we can continuously allow the obstructions to pass and resume balance.

Sun Tzu warns us that there are Five Interruptions that will work like an army to keep us from getting free of the body/material world, to the next expansion of consciousness and ultimate freedom (or unity) with the whole interconnected world or Wholeness. Our perception—our belief that the world is fixed—is part of what usurps our freedom. Thus, our mind is essentially "battling" to be released from this conceptualization.[10]

What is going to disrupt our focus? Our body. Our senses and feelings. Our thoughts and ideas. Our limiting beliefs. And our conscious attention to the fact we're being disturbed. Often, when we center our will with an intention or outcome, we're essentially waiting for something to happen. Or we might experience a sense of advancing, which in turn, creates a separation into a perception of a *here and there*, yet through the delicate practice of effortless-allowing, we see there is essentially nowhere to go, no outcome, and can let go of resistance and allow those interruptions to pass with ease. When we do, unity and oneness is possible.

If our senses try to win our attention, shattering our focus, we can regulate our attention by "facing them," (letting them arise without trying to stop them) and then allow them to fall away, which will "protect" or keep your expanding awareness intact. But the Five Interruptions are clever and cunning and know you, so they can anticipate your next move better than you. Thus, Sun Tzu warns you to be alert to avoid being "ambushed."

These interruptions are generating naturally—in a way, our past actions and beliefs create the next moment, so we're essentially in a cycle that we are undoing when we establish awareness. You might contemplate: if my thought-field of perception is effortlessly in balance (quiet), what kind of future will evolve next? We don't need to fight our interruptions, but can instead establish an awareness to them; if we can't be baited and

---

10   The *Guru Granth Sahib*, the sacred scripture of Sikhism, elaborates the struggle of the Five Interruptions, echoing Sun Tzu's treatise, demonstrating the widespread knowledge of similar teachings: "When you're plagued by great anxiety [(2) senses], diseases of the body [(1) body]; when you're wrapped up in worldly attachments [(3) thoughts/perceptions], sometimes feeling joy and other times sorrow [(4) shifting perceptions]; when you're wandering through the four directions and are restless [(5) conscious attention of interruptions]—if you come to remember the Supreme Lord God [Inner Sun], then your body/mind shall be soothed."

don't resist, or get attracted by the things that might appear in the field of consciousness, then we will maintain our balance and harmony more often.

During attunement of Contemplative-Awareness, you might see things that scare you or circle you with limiting beliefs that stir up fears and worries. Or you might experience the appearance of bright lights and impressive colors, or even see angels or saints, that may steal your attention—but if you remain unmoved, centered on the Inner Sun, and treat all phenomena arising like passing road signs on your journey to Wholeness, you will strengthen your focus and establish equanimity. If not, it would be like traveling on a highway and stopping for every little event—you won't (figuratively) get anywhere. The goal, if you will, is to experience your Inner Sun, unobstructed, from which Hidden Peace and Wholeness unfold.

As Sun Tzu offers us a variety of predicted obstructions, we can take note and plan ahead. We should be mindful of anything willing to take away our centered focus. Those disruptions will intensify and work really hard to get our attention. Like an army attacking, it will throw everything it has at us— but we mustn't budge. *For calmness to prevail our focus must be settled; if not, it can be usurped by the Five Interruptions.*

LESSON THREE (31–44): RESTORING HARMONY

Sun Tzu is very clear: the more you balance the mind with harmony, the more the disruptions will settle. But if you restrict those disruptions or try to control them, they will become more rooted and gain the advantage. Every worry, fear, aggravation, impatience, etc., that you experience forces you to use up the body's energy. It creates stress and disharmony. Ultimately, it pulls you into an exhaustive, distracted state, which can become a way of life, unless action is taken through asserting your will in the field of awareness.

Believe it or not, the natural state of our mind is quiet serenity and calm. We're drawing back (figuratively) to our original state of congruity with our surroundings, our reality. Our inherent awareness is sometimes described as "empty," because there is nothing driving, fighting, or resisting it. It's not just experienced in your mind, but through the layers around you—it's like that interconnected wheel that is always moving, chattering, engaging, or sensing the outer-hive, and then it ceases. It's moving, but motionless— motionless in the sense it's unfolding without force or sound; for this attribute, it is sometimes called, the "changeless."

The state of changelessness that is changing and eternal is a gentle unfolding that we recognize and grow accustomed to being part of. In the process, our awareness to others, the Whole, also grows gentle, as does our next action. We wouldn't want to be loud or unruly, or cast a vibration (movement) that would shatter the expansive, quiet stillness … the world is still in motion, but your perception shifts and you experience it as ordered, united, harmonious, cooperative, peaceful, and perfect, and will naturally want to participate at this level, centered in pure joy.

It takes gentle discipline to continue to return your Contemplative-Awareness toward effortless-allowing. The more you halt, stop, resist, or feel defeat, the harder it will be to restore your harmony. If you think you have subdued a distraction, and have done so with force, it will return in a cycle with greater strength to deter you. Continue to be vigilant. Never underestimate how prone you are to habit. Even at times when you think you're exercising freedom, you can actually be enslaved to your senses.

Never give up. Victory comes when we make the effort to contemplate deeply what is happening ceaselessly in the "battlefield" of our minds. Train your awareness with gentle discipline and soon you will gain confidence and be less impacted, creating footholds to victory.

EXPANDING YOUR FIELD OF AWARENESS

Sun Tzu is asking us to cultivate a deeper relationship with the way we experience our lives. We use words like contemplation, awareness, concentration, centering, Inner Sun, interruption, and disruptions, and can often lose the subtlety of the human experience we're living right this moment. We can essentially begin to apply the teaching of Contemplative-Awareness to expand our understanding of perception.

But it takes gentleness.

It takes the care of gentle hands, the way you would care for the very elderly or the very young, knowing every gesture, thought, word, effort, has a direct impact on us and others. To scold or reprimand, to find fault with our effort, can create an impression or impact that is unkind, unloving, and unproductive, among other things. That deep groove forms an obstruction on our field of awareness when we are harmful to others or ourselves.

The ability to see how hurtful we are to ourselves often eludes us. We don't often see how we can punish, harm, advocate for ill-will and misfortune on most occasions. We're very quick to forecast futures with the worst outcomes, based on scarcity and lack, and think nothing of denying ourselves our inner dreams and earnest efforts. In many ways, we are last on our list, even if we think we are acting in our best interest.

When we begin to look at the one talking and acting (the Observer) and see how those thoughts/actions are repetitively creating our "outer" world, our future, we start to see who the villain really is. It is rarely other people doing anything to us, but rather our unregulated mind forming scenarios that bring us into a perceived battle with our surroundings.

Imagine, for a moment, it's midnight and you hear a knock on the door of your home. It wakes you from sleep. In the dark, you wonder who it can be. The knocking is hard and aggressive. You listen more closely and you can hear voices, lots of them. You don't dare move, for fear of who it could be—your mind might use your history, your experiences, your sense of lack and unworthiness, your misfortunes, etc., to create the answer to who is knocking ...

Who is knocking at the door?

It's truly up to you. How you perceive the world will determine your answer. In so many words, your mind will predict and try to establish who it is, creating resistance in the way of disruption, fear, worry, surprise, aggravation, etc. For example, if you rescue animals, the knock might be someone who found a lost pet. If you ordinarily feel threatened by the people in your neighborhood, it could be them after something.

Even if the person knocking leaves, and you never went to look, you can easily be agitated by the experience for the next hour, turning over in your mind what you should've done, or dwelling on who it might've been. This can carry onto the next day, as you get to work and share the story. *It scared me right out of bed! No, I didn't go see—for all I know, they had the wrong house, and were out there with baseball bats!*

In all of these scenarios, we have the ability to gently temper the mind not to get carried away, to recognize the swaying emotion of fear or worry. The uncertainty is not real but a felt emotion (a disturbance) and we *can* bring our attention back to center, first by undertaking the strategy of concentration, then growing this to deeper contemplation, to *see* what is being thought and then not follow or get swept up by it. We must mentally remain unmoved, trusting that we will meet the moment as it unfolds.

It may not happen the first time or the tenth, but gradually, as we use our direct experiences, in each moment, as our schoolroom, we will notice how we're reacting habitually. In time, we can become aware of our own treatment of ourselves, and use this to assert a deeper level of care. We become cared for and respected; we become the one who won't put up with disharmony; we won't allow ourselves to be taken advantage of or made to feel less; we stop being second. And in those instances, when we are impacted by the exterior world—or rather, by the thoughts and actions of others—Sun Tzu explains that if we're grounded in Wholeness, we have the power to withstand any attack and not be impacted.

Our inner teacher becomes our constant companion, guiding our gentle steps. It's not that we become selfish, but that we include our own needs and care in the process of expansion. In doing so, we give more everywhere, because we are no longer disharmonious inwardly or with our environments (unity evolves); our thoughts and actions aren't careless or distracted to cause harm to anyone, *including* ourselves.

Ultimately, as our ever-expansive Contemplative-Awareness grows, the distractions lessen and we begin to trust ourselves. This is when the hidden teacher is "heard" and known, co-creating a new way of accord, a path of gentle discipline, with heightened awareness of a deeper truth that every action, every thought matters, and we will be attentive to choose them wisely.

Such is the path that Sun Tzu lays out for us, to travel at our own pace, wherever we are, toward a victory that can not only benefit ourselves but the world circulating around us.

THE NINTH STEP ON THE HIDDEN PATH TO PEACE AND WHOLENESS

1. *Apply the Hidden Path to Peace and Wholeness in whatever way best reveals itself to you to expand your Contemplative-Awareness right now.*

2. *Recognize opportunities, moment to moment, to go deeper into recognizing the habits that masquerade in your life. Pinpoint areas—at home, work, play—where you consistently end up with outcomes that are not fortuitous, but feel like they are holding you back. Contemplate how your own thoughts, about your life create the cycle and take responsibility.*

3. *Start with one area of your life to bring a deeper awareness and focus to. Each day, spend time contemplating how you arrived at this moment and what you would like your future to be. Allow your obstructing thoughts/ senses, the way your body or your surroundings disrupt you, to pass, and make new changes. Expand your awareness through direct experience, allow the Observer time to center and maintain a clear awareness that grows, bringing a deeper interconnection into your life.*

Contemplative-Awareness Expansion is the ninth step on the Hidden Path to Peace and Wholeness. The more you can know the Five Interruptions, investigate them and understand how they disrupt your momentum, and steal your quietude, the more likely you can make different choices, reassert your will, and gain the advantage.

Soon, your Inner Sun will be a natural place for you to reside, whether your eyes are opened, closed, or in sleep (as they are all one).

Let deep contemplation be a new gentle discipline to usher harmony into your life.

Ruminations: Contemplative-Awareness Expansion

"If you anchor your attention firmly, your awareness will be free of the illusory suffering experienced by the body, and this will spell victory."

– Chapter 9

----

1. Journal the events of your day and pick one where you sensed your focus diverted. In what ways can you take responsibility for the outcome and make changes for the future?

----

2. Share a time where you experienced your awareness expanding and what it felt like. What methods can you employ in the next moment to grow your awareness again to experience this effortless, boundless joy?

----

3. Pick one of the Five Interruptions that gives you the most trouble. Investigate it and with foreknowledge and gentleness discover ways you might regain control of your awareness.

----

4. Spend fifteen minutes today centered on your Inner Sun (eyes open or closed) and report your discoveries.

5. What were some of the over-ruling thoughts that disrupted your Contemplative-Awareness and what might you learn through concentration to help you let them pass freely?

6. Describe a time when you experienced a great quiet—when your mind wasn't chattering and your sense of the world seemed very silent. If you have yet to experience this, try to expand your Contemplative-Awareness now and write about it. Either way, share the characteristics of what you felt like.

7. Share a time recently that you caught your mind wandering due to one of the Five Interruptions, and how you were able to disrupt the thought and return to your center of focus.

8. Create a list of your over-ruling thoughts that were derived from limiting beliefs (like scarcity, unworthiness, etc.), and investigate through contemplation how you arrived at this as your reality. Through gentle care, how can you maintain awareness and bring about new ideas and a more intuitively-inspired future?

9. What does self-care look like and what one step can you take to welcome it into your life?

10. What does *mindful* self-care look like and what one step can you take to welcome it into your life?

11. Name three limiting beliefs you have that routinely disturb your ever-expanding awareness.

12. Share three things you've always wanted to do, but never believed you could, and what mental ruminations have disrupted your natural sense of purpose to keep you from doing them? What will you do next to fulfill even one of these?

10

TERRITORY
OF THE MIND[1]

1. Sun Tzu said: we may distinguish the Six Unfoldings[2] of the territory of the mind. They are:

a. Unfolding conscious thoughts that emerge as penetrable, easy to pass through (*accessible ground*).
b. Unfolding conscious thoughts that emerge as entwined or deceiving (*entangled ground*).
c. Unfolding perceived-thoughts that emerge as evasive, stalling, either through procrastination or indecision (*temporizing ground*).
d. Unfolding perceived-thoughts that emerge as hyper-focused, restrictive, often through reactionary effects (*narrow passes*).
e. Unfolding thought-streams that emerge as hurdles, steep and difficult to overcome, often unanticipated (*precipitous heights*).
f. Unfolding thought-streams that emerge on the outskirts of consciousness, outlying, secluded, cut off (*positions at a great distance*).

2. A conscious thought that can be traversed by awareness and disengaged on its own accord is called penetrable (mind).

---

1   *Territory of the Mind* is more specifically rendered as "the unfolding nature of the mind."
2   "Unfolding" is used here to denote the motion involved in the way the different types of thought appear in our field of conscious and intuitive perception. Likewise, the use of "conscious thought," "perceived-thoughts," and "thought-streams," are intended to offer the reader different ways to express the same idea, one that is limited by language. All are discussed further in the chapter.

3. When thoughts of this nature are penetrating the field of conscious thought, keep your Concentrated-Awareness—your attention—centered on the Inner Sun, and guard your vital energy. Then you will be able to "fight" (or maintain your position) with an advantage.

4. A conscious thought that can be abandoned (or left), yet makes it difficult to re-settle, is called entangling (mind).

5. When thoughts of this nature are entwining (or deceiving) the field of conscious thought, you can gently assert Concentrated-Awareness to maintain focus if they are still weak. But if the enemy-entwined thought is strengthened (given attention) and you cannot prevent the thought from taking root, and essentially lose concentration, it will end in disaster.

6. A conscious thought that is unable to leave but stays pivoting your attention, often through your own procrastination, is called evasive (mind).

7. When thoughts of this nature bait your attention, it is best to lure the full nature of the thought-thread to enable you to "see" it clearly, so that you can regain the advantage with Concentrated-Awareness.

8–9. With regard to hyper-focused thoughts, if you can actively settle them first, you can avoid a stronghold of resistance; you will also gain the advantage by letting the hyper-sensations settle, letting them "pass," dissipate, or become weakened.

10. With regard to a conscious thought that emerges on the outskirts of your field of conscious perception, if you know (as soon as it appears) that it has the power to be injurious to your concentration, don't pull it in closer (by thinking about it) and thereby make it accessible, but rather, keep your focus on your Inner Sun and wait to see if it will arise and pass on its own.

11. (In all the situations discussed), if the enemy-of-thought has occupied your field of conscious perception ahead of your Concentrated-Awareness, don't follow the stream of thought, but retreat and allow it to pass.

12. If, while deeply focused, a thought emerges (what feels like) very far away in the plain of consciousness, and your Concentrated-Awareness, paired with your vital energy, is equal in strength to what's arising, it may not be easy to assert your will over the thought-stream and you could end up at a disadvantage, losing your center and determination.

13. These six principles on unfolding conscious thoughts are connected to the Earth (or the body/Yang nature/Lower Consciousness).

14. Now, Concentrated-Awareness that is exposed to the Six Setbacks of conscious thought, rather than arising from one's own natural intuition, means the Observer is out of balance. The six most common ways the Concentrated Observer can end up with an imbalanced mind is:

    a. Escapism, daydreams, giving up (*flight*).
    b. Stubbornness, obstinacy, unyielding inability to change (*unbending*).
    c. Overwhelm, losing self-control, grief (*collapse*).
    d. Sense of failure, unworthiness (*ruin*).
    e. Sense of mental turmoil, pandemonium, disruption/disorder, mental upheaval, disorganized or frenzied thinking (*chaos*).
    f. Utter and crushing mental defeat (*rout*).

15. *Escapism* (or giving in to daydreams) occurs when the Observer attempts to establish concentration when the "enemy"-of-thought is great in strength (restless even); like facing an army that's ten times bigger in size, it will be hard to regain balance, and the mind will escape or avoid, rather than face the perceived difficulty.

16. When thought-streams are too strong and the concentrated-will is too weak, the ability to center awareness will face a *stubborn inability to change,* and possibly even be *overwhelmed,* stalling a return to balance.

17. If the field of consciousness is experiencing a state of anger that will not easily settle, the Observer, while trying to center awareness, will be surprised at how rancorous and unruly the thought-streams can quickly become. This takes away the advantage and surrenders to a *sense of failure and unworthiness.*

18. When Concentrated-Awareness is weak and without authority (will), when any attempt to "command" or center attention is half-hearted or not strong, when there is no initiative or strategies in place, and the mind is unruly and frenzied, the result is *utter pandemonium.*

19. When Concentrated-Awareness is unable to predict the strength of a thought-stream, it allows "inferior" habits to rule over the usually stronger volition. This overthrows the Observer's centered-focus because they have neglected to establish concentration and the result is *crushing defeat.*

20. These are the six ways of risking harmony, which must be carefully noted by the student who has established equanimity.

21. Sensing naturally occurring intuition is the student's ally. But the power to estimate the enemy-of-thought and how to gently unfold the potential limitations that risk harmony; the ability to calculate (with foreknowledge) the complexities, mental disharmonies, and intrusions possible—that is what constitutes a master.

22. The one who knows these things, and in engaging puts their knowledge into practice, will win victory (Wholeness). Those who know them not, nor practice them, will remain in a mental state of disharmony.

23. The wise know that victory over thoughts/senses is won through the command of the will alone. Whether drawn to engage or not engage thoughts/senses—whether victory is possible or not—the will is the sole authority and must be obeyed.

24. The master who advances the strength of their will without coveting self-importance and retreats from society without fearing being unpopular; whose only thought is to protect (maintain) their inner peace and harmony and be in good and gentle service to others, is the jewel of the kingdom (universe).[3]

25. Regard your will like a child and it will grow strong and harmonize with your intuition, and be with you even through the transition of earthly death.

---

3   The kingdom or "universe," the Eternal All or Whole.

26. If the student permits the thought-streams to go undisciplined, the will cannot assert control (or Concentrated-Awareness), the emotions will go unchecked without discipline and create mental disorder. In those circumstances the will (or volition) is like a spoiled child and is useless for any practical purpose in establishing centered awareness.

27. If we exercise our will, acting contrary to our limiting thought/belief, and try anyway, even though *we will fail*, we're halfway to victory.

28. If we exercise our will, acting contrary to our limiting thought/belief, but try anyway, even if *we only partially succeed*, we're halfway to victory.

29. If we exercise our will, acting contrary to our limiting thought/belief, and believe we are able to succeed, but know the conditions (e.g., physical, mental) may not make success possible, we're still near to victory.

30. Hence the experienced student is never bewildered (or afraid to risk failure) once in motion; once they have acted on their intuition, they are never at a loss.

31. Hence the saying: if you know the challenge and yourself, your victory (over any limitation) will not stand in doubt; if you know Heaven (Yin) and Earth (Yang), and know your mind with Wholeness, you make your victory complete.

INTERPRETING THE LIVING WISDOM OF SUN TZU

At this stage, Sun Tzu allows us to put our preliminary experiences of working with the mind to a much deeper practice. If we've been doing a little at a time—observing and interrupting our thoughts, getting to know our mind and how it works in each moment, questing and questioning—we can find we are making subtle progress, even if it doesn't seem like it. But even if we sense we're overcoming aspects of ourselves, a new thought can easily announce itself, like a gong strike, and reverberate in our field of awareness to possibly disrupt our thoughts.

At the same time, we also need to be mindful that thoughts aren't bad or terrible. They *just are*. Kosho Uchiyama Roshi calls them *secretions*,[4] and relates them to any other bodily substance: in the same way the nose secretes mucus, or the ears wax, the mind secretes thoughts. What a freedom, to look at thoughts neutrally, as a common function, not something to be rid of.

So while we're using common language to engage a conversation about how thoughts appear, we need to remember they are only disrupting our harmony if we allow it (or ascribe a thought to it that it is so). We're in a state of gentle-awareness, a serene harmony, and then a thought/ emotion will arise ... if we perceive it as unruly or intrusive, it can take our focus and actually *be* unruly or intrusive. But in essence, thoughts are merely coming and going, as part of what is natural, and we can equally not intrude, with attention or focus, and allow them to go from our field of thought, just as naturally.

Sun Tzu offers a precise layout of where and how our thoughts are operating and unfolding. (Chapter 11 expands on this further.) We should be encouraged, because the more knowledge we have, the more we can sense the expansion of our awareness, experience its limitlessness, and establish great lengths of harmony. Calm and peace become the norm—so much so, that we will notice the intrusion of a thought or concept much more easily. And to guide the way is the understanding of how thoughts/ concepts/ideas, images, etc., will gently appear and can possibly divert our will and attention.

---

4   See *How to Cook Your Life: From the Zen Kitchen to Enlightenment* (Shambhala Publications, 2005), pp. 28–9.

LESSON ONE (1–13): THE SIX TYPES OF THOUGHTS

Sun Tzu offers us the Six Unfoldings as a method of sensing and growing receptive to how perception evolves as a changing field through which we experience existence. We have emerging thoughts that we can easily *penetrate* and allow to fall away; then we have types of thoughts that we sense as being *entwined* and able to deceive us even though we might not think they will get stuck. We have thoughts or perceptions that *emerge* in the field of conscious thought and are evasive, stalling, procrastinating, or indecisive, staying... going... but all the same in that they can steal our inner concentration.

At times, we will experience thought emerging as hyper-focused and restrictive, with a sense of being very narrow. We often react to this type of thought, wanting relief from whatever caused it. We also have thoughts that emerge like hurdles—you know the ones that seem steep and difficult to overcome; we can't anticipate them, so they are fierce and disturb our peace of mind. But there are also thoughts that seem to appear on the outskirts of consciousness, outlying, secluded, like they aren't going to win our attention unless we make a point of ruminating on them, which ultimately "pulls" them closer.

Remember, the field of perception, as explained by Sun Tzu, is the territory of the unfolding mind, and how thoughts come into conscious focus, are/are not engaged and go. We are essentially using words to give this "field" a form, when it actually doesn't have one. That said, you can sense your thoughts "near" or "far." You can sense when they feel narrow and up close, all-consuming. Equally, you can sense your consciousness free of obstructions, in flow, open and serene—in this case, at first, you might question why you *aren't* thinking, and actually "pull" thoughts to you. It's like that when you think of something, just for a moment, and it seems like not a big deal, *until it is!* So remember, the "battlefield" and positions of thought (in the territory of the mind) are to help you gain new awareness of the way the mind is naturally in flux generating thoughts, which if grasped and focused on, will break the equanimity of conscious-unity.

Sun Tzu goes on to explain that to deal with the array of thoughts, we can better control our mind and clear the "battlefield" when we recognize the patterns of thought, as they appear in our field of perception, and even more importantly, how they appear in the *same places*, with the *same characteristics*. This gives us the foreknowledge to do "battle." For example, if you sense a thought teetering on the brink (of the field of perception), and are aware that it is "this type" of thought, which you know can divert your focus, you *cannot* focus on it. It's that simple.

The surest way to a calm, balanced mind is by maintaining Concentrated-Awareness: a mind centered on the Inner Sun, which in turn, casts a wider glow of will and unity into the boundless field of perception. Disengaging thoughts helps us "grow" our inner light. Sun Tzu is reminding us that we're already experiencing an aware, united presence, but since everything is changing—because we have lived so long with an unregulated mind—we have opportunities to deepen our connection and not be swayed by the disorder.

But even if we *are* swept away, the Inner Sun is shining, always ready and available. Some of life's most "difficult" times offer us the same opportunity to sense and receive balance (and information/guidance) from our intuition; we're simply making it easier to experience life (or our perception of it) without interference.

As Sun Tzu explains, when we can't "abandon" a thought, it makes it difficult to disentangle the perception. When our thoughts are entwined, we can assert deeper concentration to regain focus, or it can end in disaster, entwining more. Thoughts will bait us, until they become something we can't shake, leading to a state of hyper-focus, until all peace seems shattered.

Eventually, it may seem like we're fighting a war in our minds and that our thoughts have a stronghold that we can't weaken. Even thoughts that seem harmless, as they appear *far away*, can suddenly get closer and take us into a mental skirmish for control. Before we know it, we're suddenly far from the inner peace and tranquility we had a minute ago!

In all these situations, if we don't follow or fixate on our thoughts, they will pass. If a thought emerges, we can assert Concentrated-Awareness, and quell it before or at the onset of arising, so as not to lose our center, our determination... again, this is happening in every moment, not simply at a special time that we set aside from "life."

As you are going about your day, watch your mind/thoughts. Become aware of how they appear in different areas of perception. Know them and anticipate what will come next. If you get a thought arising on the fringe, and you have the foreknowledge it can take away your concentration, assert your will. Refocus your awareness to center on your Inner Sun. The more you do this, the more you clear the field of perception and strengthen your will, which can carry you to victory.

LESSON TWO (14–20): THE WILL AS THE HIGHEST AUTHORITY

Sun Tzu offers us the foreknowledge of recognizing and discerning the six ways we risk inner harmony (*flight*, *unbending*, *collapse*, ruin, chaos, and rout or defeat). The more we grow aware of what is going to impede our connection to our intuition (Wholeness), the more likely we can eliminate the cycle of imbalance again. We do this through maintaining the valued seat of concentration to regulate our field of perception.

What are we looking for? Escapism, daydreams; stubbornness, obstinacy, or an unyielding inability to change; overwhelm, losing our self-control, grief; sense of failure, unworthiness; sense of mental turmoil, pandemonium, disruption/disorder, mental upheaval, disorganization, or frenzied thinking. And then lastly, utter and crushing mental defeat.

Take a moment to ruminate how we can risk losing inner harmony through each of the Six Setbacks. Identify where and how, in your life, these can continue to keep you at a disadvantage. We must assert our will. It's like when you want to quit a habit and you think, *oh maybe just once more, why not?* The answer is that the small moment you take a command from the body, you weaken your will. You will essentially get more of the same you—the same thoughts—rather than creating a new cycle, a new you free of mental hindrances, a person centered and glowing powerfully with the strength of unity of your Inner Sun.

When we "knowingly" go along with our patterns of thought, we're giving up our free will and volition, surrendering the battlefield, shaking our determination, and risk ushering in different mental states that could lead to pandemonium. The stronger your volition, the more you will overthrow the habit/thought and the more you will keep making progress toward gaining a foothold to maintain equanimity more of the time (and eventually, *all of the time*).

Even when it seems like a thought is *no big deal*, we need to recognize the costs of engaging old habits/thought patterns or allowing our emotions to assert power over our will. To this end, we have only to willfully try again and then act with determination.

LESSON THREE (21–25): THE POWER OF INTUITION

Our inherent gift, our greatest ally, is our naturally occurring intuition—one we should never underestimate. It is working, even when we feel lost and hopeless. The more we can attune to, or tap into it, and allow it to unfold and emerge, the more likely intrusions will find it impossible to unseat our concentration.

We basically establish a felt-sense of *what is* and lose our ability to doubt, because we have a deep-knowing beyond words or circumstances. It's like when you decide, for some seemingly random reason, not to do something, only to find out later that you avoided danger. That's the power of intuition, available to us all the time. The more we can tap into it, the more our lives flow; we're interrupted less. In theory, with our intuition as the highest voice of authority, thoughts reduce, since we're less likely to be consumed with doubt, worry, fear, etc., which has been replaced with "Constant-Knowing."

Even when an experience we might deem difficult or "bad" erupts, we are—guided by Intuitive-Knowing—more likely to perceive it with understanding, as part of our natural Wholeness, and necessary to our potential growth.

We can falsely believe that the disquieted mind is normal, but it's actually serenity that is. As we strive to become aware of the territory of the mind, we see a little goes a long way. You will have days of mental quiet, when the tiniest thing will attempt to stir it, but you will not want it to and guard against the intrusions. In fact, you begin to see the numerous ways that disruption is possible and you stop opening your field of perception to it.

As you maintain the stronghold of concentration to preserve your mental serenity and balance, you need to act upon the decision of the will with determination. Acting half-heartedly will only get you half-concentration. So put your whole heart into it!

As Sun Tzu explains, the one who advances the strength of their will without coveting self-importance and retreats from society without fearing being unpopular; whose only thought is to protect (maintain) their inner peace and harmony and be in good and gentle service to others,[5] is the jewel of the kingdom (universe), the Master Sun. The more we act upon the will, the less likely we are to fail or doubt, allowing it to guide our lives. Then we will essentially care-take our will as we would a child, tenderly and protectively.

LESSON FOUR (26–31): THE CYCLES OF CHALLENGES

Because thoughts are in flux and circulating across the field of perception, much the same way cake batter churns in ripples in a mixer, we will have moments of feeling victory and then moments when we will need to

---

5   Broadly speaking, when we regulate our minds, our field of perception, to a state of equanimity, our inner peace is felt by others, and essentially, in "good and gentle service" to others, since they are no longer impacted by our distraction/disturbance, judgment, disharmony, etc.

overcome something winning our attention. Habits, limitations, unresolved emotions (for example, the past, past lives), can cycle back like webs of memory, and when left unchecked, can create mental disorder.

For example, if you are afraid of public speaking and asserted your will to overcome it, you could easily find yourself regularly speaking in front of crowds successfully—maybe even making a career of it. But then, a year or more could go by, and since the field of perception is always changing and moving through cycles, you could easily find the emotional response returned, and you're once more afraid to take the stage again. You might be on stage, mentally *unafraid*, while the body responds with flutters.

Since the field of perception continues to evolve and churn up old emotions and thoughts through memory,[6] *that which was mastered* can present itself again, mentally or even physically—you might even feel the energy stuck in the body, and through your determined will (to not be afraid to speak publicly), you can restore your balance. Energy exercises, like tai-chi or qigong, can free stuck memory from the body, and the energy associated with it, to restore balance.

Ultimately, it is your determined will and action that influences your chances to win victory. Even if we know we will fail, we try anyway. Even if we know there is a *possibility* that we might *half*-fail, we try anyway. Partial success is winning. Every time we assert our will to overcome something, we are gaining ground. The key is to act upon the will and not weaken it with half-hearted attempts. Since our intuition is always present and guiding us, we can trust our inherent wisdom and not be afraid to risk failure.

To this end, we can fail challenges but still know without doubt that we are one step closer to our victory.

KNOWING THE UNFOLDING MIND

Sun Tzu is offering us a view of the ever-expanding conscious-awareness, *the territory of the unfolding mind*. It's easier to look at this as a battlefield, or an area that can be traversed, versus an intangible, unseen concept that we have no control over. We very much *do* have control! That said, when we explore the "territory" of the mind—or the Nine (Impartial) Fields of Perception (see Chapter 11)—we're discussing simple matters about where

---

6   Memory, as explained by Sun Tzu, includes the imprint of energy within the body's cells, past lives, or historical memory.

thoughts "appear" in your conscious perception of your mind, how they come in cycles, go, stay, or connect—how they can or don't disturb your normal state of equanimity.

So right now, let's pause for a moment and tune in to the territory you know or sense as your mind. Where is your mind? Where are your thoughts occurring? (Not in your head, but somewhere open and spacious—perhaps around you.) As you sense your mind/thoughts, you might experience silence. Now wait for a thought to come. Do you have it? Point to it. Where are you sensing that particular thought arising—front, back, side, over there?

That "area" or "territory" where the thought is materializing is what we are going to explore and master. It's a really wonderful method of recognizing that the thoughts are not limited and located in your head or your body, but they are boundlessly forming (figuratively) around you—sometimes in what is called the quantum field—or space or Heaven. St. Teresa likened it to Solomon's temple, "during which no noise could be heard," as she experienced the deepest silence and ascended ordinary reality.[7]

Why this is important is because we don't need to be fancy when talking about the *thing* we're communicating; our thoughts are not locked up in our head, and when you begin to discuss where your thoughts are with another person, you will see your thought is right next to someone else's! Their perception is aligned with yours because there are no boundaries. When you can sense thought outside yourself, you will begin to interpret this field more readily and anticipate the way thought moves, like an army, into your field of awareness. That's why we can feel and sense the consciousness of others, or sometimes know what others are thinking even before they say it. This ability only gets stronger.

How do we develop this understanding? We simply can engage in our day-to-day lives aware of the Six Setbacks. Take time to look at the list and understand how each of them has played a part in your thought processes. *Know yourself.* Know ahead of time how you "escape" or "daydream" to avoid dealing with difficulties, for example, and then actively and willfully be attentive when you do it again. Make changes. Assert your will even when you know you'll fail. Then next time it will get easier. Keep trying and never give up. Once you master one of the Six Setbacks, move on to the next, and keep winning battles, asserting your will and concentration.

---

7   Seventh Mansion, Chapter 2, *The Interior Castle*.

The goal is to recognize that thoughts aren't as powerful as we've been led to believe. Something that always bothered you can be swept away with love and serenity. We eventually sustain a mental field of calm, which is harmonious and in balance, and the "secretions"—the natural thoughts—lessen; or when they do appear, they don't have the strength to pull you away from your calm. You actually *know* better.

THE TENTH STEP ON THE HIDDEN PATH TO PEACE AND WHOLENESS

1. *Apply the Hidden Path to Peace and Wholeness in whatever way best reveals itself to you to attune to the territory of the mind right now.*

2. *Recognize opportunities, moment to moment, to attune to your intuition and sense the way forward, through the Six Unfoldings, to eliminate the duality of thought and worry. Even in difficulty, try to sense your calm awareness right behind the emotions and senses. Notice how and "where" thought is appearing, so as to know ahead of time the "type" of thought and how it will act and evolve. This will give you the confidence to stay concentrated.*

3. *Notice moments throughout the day when you can recognize yourself entertaining one of the Six Setbacks. Try to assert your will and recenter your concentration. Allow thoughts to come and go, without giving them a reason to develop a stronger foothold. Be mindful of your own ability to say "no" to usual thought patterns and habits to overcome your own limitations. Make harmony and calm the central focus, even when it seems like you might fail.*

Territory of the Mind is the tenth step on the Hidden Path to Peace and Wholeness. The more you can know the Six Unfoldings and the Six Setbacks, the more likely you will be to create new ideas and outcomes for your life. Observe and address your mental thought patterns as they arise in the field of perception. Sense where they occur, and be willing to "allow" and "regulate" by applying the Gentle-Way of observation. Act contrary to your limiting thought/belief and make protecting (maintaining) your inner peace the highest priority, in good and gentle service to others.

Ruminations: Territory of the Mind

"The student who has established equanimity must take note of the six ways of risking harmony."

– Chapter 10

---

1. Pick one of the Six Unfoldings of the territory of the mind and share an example of where you have experienced the type of thought explained (for example, accessible, entwined, etc.) and how it swept you away.

---

2. Pick another one of the Six Unfoldings of the territory of the mind and share an example of where you have experienced the type of thought explained (for example, accessible, entwined, etc.) and how you overcame it.

---

3. When a thought appears on the fringes of your perception, it may feel far away, but no less able to be drawn into closer focus to win your attention. Consider a thought-stream that was not really on your radar, which you pulled in, and then the results—if you were able to see it flow away or if it distracted you.

---

4. Center your attention and observe your thoughts, then draw a map of your field of perception, to demonstrate where some of the reoccurring thoughts may have appeared. What can be learned by it?

5. Pick one of the Six Setbacks and share your experience of how your harmony was disrupted. In hindsight, was there a way to avoid it?

6. Pick one of the Six Setbacks and share your experience of how your harmony was NOT disrupted. In hindsight, what did you do to maintain equanimity?

7. Of the Six Setbacks, which is the one that gives you the most difficulty to maintain your harmony? Or the least?

8. Share an example of where you were able to notice your naturally occurring intuition and how it worked with your will to create a harmonious/calm mind or solution to a situation.

9. Name a time when you knew you were going to fail but tried anyway and were better for it. Name a time where you exercised your will contrary to your limiting belief/habit and were the better for it.

10. Share a time when you set out to do something—for example, to achieve a goal—and halfway to completing it, you didn't think you could succeed, but you tried anyway. What lesson can you take away from this and apply going forward?

11. Share a time your intuition has served you in overcoming difficulty.

12. Ruminate the following passage and write a short paragraph about what it means to you. "If you know the challenge and yourself, your victory (over any limitation) will not stand in doubt; if you know Heaven (Yin) and know Earth (Yang) to know your mind with Wholeness, you may make your victory complete."

THE NINE (IMPARTIAL) FIELDS OF PERCEPTION

1. Sun Tzu said: the art of mastering conscious-unity and equanimity recognizes Nine Fields of Perception, which are neither good nor bad but impartial: (a) scattered; (b) non-resistant; (c) the few unseat the many; (d) vast, without need of retreat; (e) crisscrossing; (f) protracted; (g) obtrusive; (h) encircling; (i) hollowed.

2. When thoughts (images/concepts/ideas) appear in the field of perception scattered and split up, you will sense them in your immediate field of awareness *sprinkled and strewn about* to win or evade your attention.

3. When thoughts appear in the field of perception as non-resistant and permeable, you will sense them in your local field of awareness at *no great distance*, coming and going defiantly in cycles like ocean waves, either to win or steal the advantage.

4. When thoughts appear in the field of perception as few in number, they can easily unseat (*the many*) your strong concentration. You will sense them in your localized field of awareness as neutral or not a concern, stalling to steal your focus; so don't be fooled—either side can win the advantage.

5. When thoughts (images/concepts/ideas) appear in the field of perception as if a vast field with no need to retreat, communicating easily and connecting freely with other images/concepts/ideas, you will sense them emerging in your local and distant range of awareness, creating mental networks that are neutral—until they're not.

6. When thoughts appear in the field of perception converging and crisscrossing, you will sense them emerging in your local and distant range of awareness, creating an entanglement (that is essentially neutral until given attention)—whoever gets the advantage first (concentration or mental disorder), gains the full Empire.

7. When thoughts appear in the field of perception as neither retreating nor advancing, but no less critical, alarming, worrying, or grievous, you will sense them emerging in your local *and* distant range of awareness, as protracted—or stretched out—*hostile* even, if concentration is lost.

8. When thoughts appear in the field of perception as obtrusive (combative), burdening concentration and dividing it, you will sense them emerging in your local *and* distant range of awareness, as seemingly mountainous, difficult to summit—which is neutral until centered awareness becomes imbalanced.

9. When thoughts appear in the field of perception as surrounding and restricting, you will sense them as "circling" your immediate range of awareness, which is neutral—until it's not.

10. When thoughts appear in the field of perception as if your focus, let alone your concentration, is devoid or impermissible, you will sense it as a "narrow, deep hollowed valley" in your immediate range of awareness, which could easily emerge as overwhelm or a sense of hitting rock-bottom, if focus/concentration is lost.

11. Therefore, when perceiving thoughts as "scattered" or "split up," don't engage them. If perceiving thoughts as non-resistant, coming and going, don't stop to give them any notice; when perceiving thoughts that seem like only a few (that *could* overtake your focus), don't engage them either.

12. When perceiving thoughts in the vast and open field of awareness, don't try to block their evolution. If your field of perception seems like your thoughts are crisscrossing, join your concentration with joy and effortless love.

13. When perceiving thoughts that emerge as protracted and stretched out, gather your full volition to overcome, and reestablish your concentration. If experiencing thoughts that are obtrusive, keep your concentration steadily moving on.

14. When your perception is hyper-focused, with thoughts that are sensed as encircling your field of awareness, resort to a stratagem (see Chapter 3); when the (impartial) thoughts you perceive have your field of awareness involved with a narrow, deeply grooved, hollowed focus, fight to regain your concentration.

15. Those (ancients) who were called skilled Observers over the impartial field of perception knew how to drive a wedge between the advancing thought-stream and effortlessly assert Concentrated-Awareness to create cooperation between (the perceived differences between) disorder/concentration and (the perceived differences between) low/high consciousness; and keep impartial thoughts from hindering the presence of harmony/peace, to rally the seat of equanimity (Inner Sun).

16. When thought-streams are scattered, they prevent the Observer from concentrating; even when conscious-awareness is united, they manage to keep the field of perception in disorder.

17. When thought-streams have the advantage, they continue forward, multiplying, when otherwise they would be still—or united with the whole awareness.

18. If asked how to cope with a great host of orderly thoughts on the verge of creating imbalance to inner harmony, seize the advantage by asserting your will over the true nature of the thought.

19. Rapidity is the essence of mental war: take advantage of the opportunity when your thoughts are still weak and can be allowed to pass effortlessly.

20. The following are the principles to be observed regarding an invading thought-stream: the further your concentration (or calculated attention) penetrates into the Nine (Impartial) Fields of Perception, the greater your volition will be, and so the invading thoughts will not prevail in unseating your equanimity.

21. Take time to "resupply" through Contemplative-Awareness to maintain your vitality, your Inner Sun.

22. Carefully examine (contemplate) your focus, your will, your centered concentration, and don't overtax them. Concentrate your vital energy and store your strength. Keep your mind in a state of readiness (over laxity) and devise immeasurable "plans" (see Chapter 1) to maintain your seat of power (equanimity).

23. Put your volition out into the field of thought, knowing there is no retreat to old habits and patterns, and be willing to express a "no return" strategy to overcome any limitation. If you can, there is nothing you won't be able to do (or overcome), and your body/mind/spirit will be whole, strengthened, and invigorated (a great healing will take place).

24. Habits/repeating cycles of thought will become desperate/stubborn to keep rooted in the field of perception. If there is no refuge, they will get more difficult and unafraid to "attack" your concentration.

25. Thus, without waiting to be marshaled, the Concentrated-Awareness will be alert, attentive/present, maintaining a faithful presence and obedience to keep order and balance in the regions of the mind.

26. Prohibit the illusion of omens and superstitious-doubts that your ego (ordinary self) will be lost. This way, when the field of perception is clear, a great distress won't be feared.

27–30. If our "soldiers" of awareness are not overburdened by the beliefs of gain and loss, but can overcome their perception of reality with courage, they will recognize the strength in cutting off the thought at the root, as soon as it arises, before it can spread (permeate), or rouse your awareness. It is through the Gentle-Way of impartiality—*seeing all experiences as one whole, and awareness and perception not as enemies at war*—that one will experience a constant presence of Wholeness, as the ultimate perceivable reality.

31. Hence, it is not enough to put one's trust in the gathering of senses and the burrowing of emotions into the mutable field of perception.

32. Courage to assert a strong will (volition) over the senses and emotions is the highest principle of awareness.

33. Revealing the ins and outs of the fields of perception, through inquiry and observation, is the best means of identifying your weak/strong points (your opportunities to marshal your perceived shortcomings).

34–37. Thus, a skillful Observer will assert Concentrated-Awareness effortlessly, like a quiet, dignified sentinel in harmony, to maintain mental order (equanimity). The Observer must be able to baffle the arising thoughts/ideas (the body, even) by imbuing a false impartiality, a carefree non-involvement. They must keep arising thoughts in ignorance, changing strategies with an aloofness, so that the enemy-of-thought will not be able to anticipate concentration's true purpose: to maintain calm-balance.

38–40. At the crucial moment the Observer exercises a clear will (volition) across the field of awareness, which cuts off the thought-streams, it's like kicking out the ladder after someone has climbed a tree, making retreat impossible. At this point, the volition has the full advantage to break rooted limitations; the business of the Observer is to ensure there is no "fuel" or "supply" for the limitation to return again.[1]

41. The different measures suited to the nine fields of awareness—the expediency of strategic-concentration and recognition of the basic limitations experienced as a result of human nature—should be readily studied.

42–51. The deeper your awareness (or the rays of the Inner Sun) can go to penetrate (with volition) the Nine (Impartial) Fields of Perception, the greater cohesion will mature. *All phenomena arising are impartial, up until the point they are regarded as intrusions.* Therefore, maintain contemplative unity; quicken alert-awareness to keep thoughts from rooting in and needing attention; be vigilant; ensure that thoughts aren't allowed to connect and multiply—consolidate them; keep your vital energy supplied; effortlessly assert your will, even when it seems like resistance is the best way to regain concentration, especially when it appears to be surrounded.

---

1   To offer a contemporary illustration, it may very much feel like a whole uninvited ghost or specter (as visibly rendered in horror movies) that had been haunting you, attached to your spirit, has now fled and vacated; it will usher in an experience of pure silence, as awareness expands in the emptiness, overcome with bliss, without the thought-stream or limitation there any longer to think about or pay attention or give energy to. You may even wonder what changed or where it has gone, but not care, embracing freedom and victory.

52. We cannot enter into alliance with harmony until we are acquainted with our entire field of perception (and all that it contains). We are not fit to lead our Concentrated-Awareness "on the march" to face our perceptions of reality until we can recognize how they are sensed/interpreted (high/broad, close-up, narrowly, distantly, intersecting, split-up, etc.) beyond what we view as ordinary reality—if we don't "see" the process of thoughts, we won't be able to create a natural advantage through effortless-allowing and centered concentration.

53–57. To be ignorant of the following principles will keep harmony from maturing: preventing thoughts from concentrating its force against the will; keeping them from multiplying; maintaining an aloof awareness so that the limitation does not anticipate its removal, making it easy to uproot it. Increase your will through joy and peace and your Concentrated-Awareness will extend to the farthest regions of perception; confront arising ideas spontaneously with volition, even if you don't think you can succeed fully.

58. Concentrated-Awareness, with a strong volition, can go anywhere in the field of perception and it will continue to expand and never be unseated.

59. It's often, when the limitations seem at their strongest, that we can assert our wills just a little more and come out the victor.

60. Success in mental warfare is gained by carefully inquiring as to the nature of our thoughts and perceptions: *Where do they come from? How were they generated? Why do I give them attention? How do I sense them? Why do the same ideas repeat and multiply? ...*

61. By persistently ruminating the nature of perception (and how thoughts appear and operate), we will succeed in the long run to take our seat of power at the Inner Sun.

62. This is called the ability to accomplish victory through calculation and cunning (reason).

63. On the day that you take your seat at the center of the field of perception (Inner Sun), block your senses, cut off the emotions, marshal the body from unseating concentration.

64. Be stern in your ability to direct your vital energy to win favor and control over the senses, emotions, and organs.

65. If a thought leaves a door open (arises), you must rush in to close it.

66. Forestall your thoughts by diverting conscious attention; contrive to keep the thought-stream from multiplying.

67. Walk in the path defined by discipline and establish an undisputed volition to break the hold of any limitation decisively.

68. At first, then, exhibit coyness, so that the thought will not anticipate your will, and automatically create a habituated response. Then rapidly cut off any chance for it to engage you by exerting your concentrated-will and you will remain unopposed.

INTERPRETING THE LIVING WISDOM OF SUN TZU

Sun Tzu offers us a method to master conscious-unity and equanimity through identifying the Nine (Impartial) Fields of Perception, which are neutral. This means that as a thought or an image appears, it is not intrinsically good or bad, only your thinking it is one way or the other makes it so. We can utilize the nine fields to see this even more clearly.

If you have a nagging thought about work, for example, it will more often reappear in the same "area" and exhibit the same emotion. Knowing this, we start to see cycles and repetitions less as things *happening* to us, but as automatically generated, and therefore, something that we're capable of monitoring and regulating. Remember, Sun Tzu assumes that we're already in a state of perfection, that the rays of our Inner Sun are permeating across our field of perception, unfolding Wholeness. The type of encounters generated through thought/image/idea will either diminish or strengthen the Inner Sun's reach.

Sun Tzu suggests that these (often) perceived obstacles are simply ruminations that arise, neither good nor not good. If we engage them (or think about what comes to mind), it'll be partly cloudy; if we are sucked in by them, storm clouds will appear; if we let them pass and not win our focus, it will be sunny. To be in full view of the Inner Sun is to experience Wholeness (or equanimity). To be partly cloudy, means your concentration and attention are imbalanced, and so on.

Further, we have nothing to obtain, nothing to rid our mind of. We can observe our mind, see how/when our thoughts arise and their texture—or how they appear to us and where we sense them. In doing so, it becomes useful for the next time, until you recognize where (figuratively) in the field of perception the thought arises and how it is sensed, to know its power and how to assert the advantage through deeper concentration.

Gradually, the more you gain knowledge of how your mind, and the thoughts it generates, works, the more you can predict your reactions; you will also see them as patterns and cycles and be less taken in by them.

LESSON ONE (1–19): SENSING AND ATTUNING TO THOUGHTS
This chapter begins to articulate the strategy we can begin to apply, in order to perceive thoughts/ideas in our boundless awareness. To recap, they are neither good nor bad, but impartial, and include (a) scattered; (b) non-resistant; (c) the few unseat the many; (d) vast, without need of retreat; (e) crisscrossing; (f) protracted; (g) obtrusive; (h) encircling; (i) hollowed.

As we've been observing our thoughts, we won't be too surprised by this information. Instead, we might feel a close kinship to our field of perception and the trueness of being able to sense our thoughts on a greater level. Even if it feels new to us to consider that our thoughts are coming and going like radio waves across an invisible field, we can apply the teaching.

Some clues Sun Tzu offers include sensing thoughts that "feel" or can be intuited in the field:

- As *sprinkled and strewn about* to win or evade your attention.

- As being at *no great distance,* coming and going defiantly in cycles, like ocean waves, to either win or steal the advantage.

- As few in number that can easily unseat your strong (*the many*) concentration.

- As if they are a *vast field,* communicating easily and connecting with other ideas/concepts, freely.

- As *converging and crisscrossing,* even entangled.

- As *protracted*—or *stretched out*—even *hostile,* if concentration is lost.

- As seemingly *mountainous,* difficult to summit.

- As *surrounding and restricting,* even encircling.

- As a *narrow, deep hollowed valley.*

When we sense and attune to our thoughts more precisely, we can engage them in different ways, so as to maintain our balance—I liken it to a contemporary example, like walking on a sidewalk in a busy town: I'm apt to encounter all types of people, activity, roving dog-walkers, noise, etc., and I wouldn't think of yelling or getting angry as a means of navigating, but I would spontaneously pivot and flow in and out of the commotion or disturbances, not missing a beat.

Sun Tzu gives us advice about how to do the same with various types of thoughts:

- With scattered or split up thoughts, don't engage them.

- When thoughts are non-resistant, coming and going, don't stop to give them any notice.

- When there are few thoughts (that *could* overtake your focus), don't engage them either.

- When thoughts feel like they are open and vast, don't try to block their flow.

- When thoughts seem to be crisscrossing, assert concentration effortlessly.

- When thoughts feel protracted and stretched out like an elastic band, assert your will to reestablish your concentration.

- When thoughts are obtrusive, keep your concentration steadily moving on.

- When your thoughts are hyper-focused, resort to a stratagem (see Chapter 3).

- When your thoughts feel narrow and deeply grooved, fight to regain your concentration.

To take these actions, Sun Tzu explains, we need to become a skilled Observer of the impartial field of perception. In so many words, the more we examine our thoughts, the more we see the states of mind we're carrying forward into each moment. So, if your thought-stream looks like a circus, so will your life; if your thought-streams looks like crisscrossing barbed wire, your life will be the same; likewise, if you have a few ruminations popping up and a steady stream of calm, your life will take on the same presence or climate.

The other key is that nothing in the field is permanent. Thoughts are travelers. We're the ones stopping them from moving on—some of us are giving them hotel stays! Remember, what feels evident and important, *may not be*, with further investigation. Likewise, all thought is impartial, so begin to tap into this wisdom, and recognize the nature of your thoughts.

The stress is on rapidity—the idea that we are working quickly before our thoughts get carried away. The more we don't react but anticipate our usual thought-stream/thought habit, the more likely it is we can master our efforts and take our consciousness to a new place where thoughts are unrestricted, allowed to come and go.

LESSON TWO (20–32): ASSERTING AND MAINTAINING VOLITION

Once we begin to sense/attune to the Nine (Impartial) Fields of Perception, we can start to further establish our concentration and attention. It's a gradual process, one where we will feel like we're advancing a little then also taking a step back. It can be likened to traveling on an escalator to the next floor: you have one leg on one step, and the other trailing below; and you are climbing in-between steps, sometimes high and low, but eventually you get to the top, with both feet landing together. One of the tools we'll use to maintain our balance and natural state of equanimity, when thoughts arise, is to assert our will—our deep volition and determination to act—so we won't destabilize.

How do we maintain our strength, our great will, to overcome the greatest difficulties? Well, of course, with the aid of our Inner Sun, which is always shining inwardly. We get to tune in at any moment and draw from our intuition, to recognize our already perfect state and reclaim our awareness of it. We "hear" and "sense" the way to go (figuratively) through our intuition, which comes effortlessly, even when our minds are in chaos or hyper-focused. It's just harder to hear. If in times of mental calm, we can "know" what our intuition sounds/feels like, then when our mind is disruptive, we're more apt to feel the nudge and end the disruption quicker.

This is why Sun Tzu advises keeping our mind flexible and in a state of readiness. We can actively lay plans and be prepared to undertake a strategy. We're constantly able to assess the "costs of (mental) war" if we get lax or lazy (or any of the other interruptions emerge). Moment to moment, we can negotiate and discern the weaknesses and strengths of the thoughts appearing; we strategize. We get to know our minds better than we know the way to the local store! Then we can incorporate the other teachings, like calculating our nature; varying our method through interrupting and diverting our thoughts—all while being rooted in concentration. And we get really good at it!

Concentrated-Awareness (or contemplation), with volition, becomes your new superpower, as you engage the emerging thoughts and sense them in the Nine Fields of (Impartial) Perception. As Sun Tzu puts it, to exhibit volition we begin to express a *"no return" strategy to overcome any limitation. There is then nothing you won't be able to do or overcome.* It's like when you say "no," and it really means NO. It's like when you see yourself saying, doing, thinking, the same patterns and you end them by pledging "no return." That's it. Done. No more. You will not let the thought or pattern retreat, only to return again for another entanglement. You're just *done.*

More tools to consider, as we assert our unstoppable will, include continuing to see thoughts with impartiality. Break their hold of being "right/wrong," or any other dualistic thinking. As we arouse our awareness, we will no longer see "enemies at war," but a continuous, constant presence, as the ultimate perceivable reality. (Exciting, right?) Therefore, we don't need to follow our senses or emotions any longer— we don't need to react the same way we have done, but can allow or assert our courageous will and create a new future forward.

LESSON THREE (33–68): CREATING AND GAINING ADVANTAGES

Our ability to assess our thoughts through inquiry and observation is the best means of identifying our weak/strong points. We become like the quiet sentinel, aloof and effortlessly watching, to anticipate what will come next in our mind; we change strategies, if needed, and maintain calm.

When the crucial moment comes to either succumb to the thought or overcome it, we can assert a clear will to cut off the thought—like kicking out the ladder after someone has climbed a tree—making retreat impossible, as we gain the advantage. We work quickly, returning to balance. But we are easy with ourselves if we can't. The rewards keep the Inner Sun shining, our intuition flowing, and our outward actions more in line with calm-balance, so as not to create more disorder.

Be wary of resisting thoughts: it may seem like we want to stop them and may get angry in doing so, but letting go is the gentle way to gain the advantage.

Lastly, as our thoughts appear to march on, and we sense and interpret them (high/broad, close-up, narrowly, distantly, intersecting, split-up, etc.), we can begin to create natural advantages through effortless-allowing and centered concentration. Even if we don't notice a thought at first as it emerges, when we do, we can confront it spontaneously with volition, even if we don't think we can succeed fully. We can go anywhere in expansive awareness and never be unseated. We must have no fear, but also be mindful of the way we can be unseated or interrupted. The key is to remember that when the limitation seems strongest, we *can* assert our will just a little more and come out the victor.

In closing, Sun Tzu provides us with more inner wisdom on the triumphs and treasures of consistently and continuously ruminating on the nature of perception, so as to know earnestly the way it operates and creates our reality, our lives. We will get so good at knowing our mind that as soon as a thought enters it, we'll meet it. "If a thought leaves a door open (arises), you must rush in to close it." It is our choice to break the hold of limitation.

PERCEPTIONS AND THOUGHTS IN DAILY LIFE

Where are your thoughts? Go ahead and point to them. They aren't in your head, but they are coalescing and churning in the infinite, boundless field of perception. What is the field of perception? Everything you're experiencing. This chapter offers you the next upgrade, so to speak, on understanding how thoughts form and "appear" in the mind.

We don't need to use fancy language or think because we're talking about science-y things that we can't grasp it or it's too lofty. No, we're all human, and experiencing the changes of thought. If we can examine them with more undertsanding than we do right now, guess what? We can begin to see how we're creating a lot of our own problems.

Ever go to take something out of the refrigerator and it ends up on the floor? And it just happens right at the time you need to leave the house in a hurry, and the last thing you need is a mess to clean up. If you view that as a negative, impatient experience, that's what it is. If you look at it closer, you dropped something. Oh well. If it was a child who dropped it— *oh my,* it could be forgiven, but a drunk friend who did it, maybe should have known better.

We can be very judgmental in situations like this, because we want life to be ordered. Yet, it's an impartial moment—something dropped. The emotion is being *added in* to make more of it and depends on the way you perceive the details (e.g., child vs. drunken friend). The more we can get involved with how we're making those determinations of bother, difficulty, hassle, mess, careless-me… which contrast to easy, happy, light, carefree, and so on, the more we can just be easy and see experiences as neutral … and that's when we just flow.

Gradually, as you recognize and *know the mind,* you move and think in harmony, not stopping to obstruct every little thing with a penalty or praise.

The core of the Nine (Impartial) Fields of Perceptions covers the ability to see where the thought is arising and then once you "know," to begin to recognize that the same type of thought appears in the same place, offering you the foreknowledge to act immediately to create changes in your perception.

For example, if you sense a thought in the outlying region (in the field of perception) or in the narrow pass, Sun Tzu lets you know *exactly* the *type* of thought that's going to show up here, and *exactly* how you will act as a result, so you can plan accordingly. The more you do, the more opportunity you have to actually create beneficial changes and substitute imbalance for a harmonious, war-free way of life. You anticipate your next thought.

If, for example, you heard news of a thief in your town staying in the mountain regions, your reaction may not be too concerned. If the thief struck again across the river, you still might not feel too bothered, but might at least ensure the doors to your house and car were locked. If the thief struck in your neighborhood, you might begin to check the doors and windows to your house/car more often. Once the thief is on your street, your concern will increase to vigilance. If the thief appears on your front porch, you would handle it right away. Of course, the thief symbolizes thought and how it appears in the field of perception: knowing where the thought appears will allow you to sense and notice its appearance, and then take the right kind of action to "handle" it.

As we begin to view reality less as being created from one thought to the next—or many thieves infiltrating our centered concentration—they will naturally diminish. In return, our future changes because our body and environment changes—the usually disordered thoughts aren't in control, our equanimous intuition is.

Sun Tzu explains that the more you assert Concentrated-Awareness across the field of perception, the more you remain in a state of readiness. So, when a new thought-stream arises (like a thief) you will more easily "know" its nature and "vanquish" it, or not give it fuel/energy of thought.

While Sun Tzu uses common landscapes to have us think about the "field" of perception, or a battlefield, we can use more contemporary images, such as how we navigate our homes, work, or neighborhoods. See the following examples to illustrate the Nine (Impartial) Fields of Perceptions. (These are only examples and are not an indication of how thoughts will appear for you; they are merely offered as a means of illustrating the principles.)

(a) *Scattered*: When you're sitting at the table working on something, whatever thought/idea is right there, up-close, in your immediate thought-field. Like if you're washing dishes, what are you thinking about? Taking out the trash, what are you thinking about? In the shower, what are you thinking about? Then what else are you *also* thinking about? In this field, thoughts are localized and scattered, as the mind flits from one idea to the next.

(b) *Non-resistant*: When there is a knock at the door, you aren't afraid or curious, or even bothered, you simply aren't interested or pulled to see who it is. But it's enough to disrupt what you were doing. For some, cellphones/technology are the contemporary "knock" at the door all day long.

(c) *The few unseat the many*: If someone goes by your window, or there is construction out in the street, or children playing, you may or may not notice. But you register the disturbances, which defiantly come and go in cycles (like ocean waves), to either win or steal the advantage.

(d) *Vast, without need of retreat*: Noises from distant streets or overhead in airplanes, also have no ability to steal your attention, unless you pull them closer. No matter what, you have the free will to discern, to engage thought, to accept distraction or not.

(e) *Crisscrossing*: This field will feel like you have a clothes line set up in your house, as your mind crisscrosses ideas/concepts. For example, the washing machine is imbalanced and making noise, while the delivery worker needs a signature; you work from home and have a call to take or are in a meeting; a loud motorcycle cruises by disturbing you; you have an argument with a family member; the water bill is due; you're hungry and have to pee; a news alert lets you know the weather is about to change and a bomb just exploded in a busy capital killing many ...

(f) *Protracted*: Thoughts in this field will feel like a long hose you are carrying in the house... and all the way to your car... and to your workplace... You are thinking: *Did I turn off the burning pot on the stove before leaving the house? I think so. Maybe I did. Why was I even cooking that dish, no one likes it. I remember when my grandmother used to make it for me... those were good times. She always made us feel special. What was her secret ingredient? I'm sure I turned the stove off—I wouldn't be that stupid... though, there was that one time... I should turn around and check... but then I'll be late. I hate being late... No, I... I don't know ...*

(g) *Obtrusive*: This field is like having an open window in the attic during an ice storm, and needing to get to it to close, but the five flights up to it are blocked with pianos! These are thoughts that are seemingly mountainous and difficult to reach, sensed usually *above* us, teetering and imposing, on our field of concentration.

(h) *Encircling*: This field is like having the dog chase the cat who's chasing a bird around the outside of your house. Thoughts circle and surround the mind, and if given the power, give a sense of being entrapped or unable to stop the loop. Mental abuse, torture, and similar, fall under this category.

(i) *Hollowed:* This field is like having a tree come through the floor of your house. The thought-stream will shoot up, narrowly, straight into your field of perception to win your *immediate* attention. As such, it can feel like you've hit rock-bottom and have no hope of getting free of the thought. Accidents, very trying situations, and traumatic events often show up in this way.

You might also liken the Nine Fields of (Impartial) Perception to different types of dogs, from small to large, that are carrying or "fetching" our thoughts and bringing them to us; or if we can assert our will, we can ask the dogs to carry them away.

The key is to be creative and use your everyday surroundings as a way to recognize that thoughts are moving, changing, shifting, and crisscrossing around you—the "field" is boundless. The more we recognize when a "clothes line" thought is being put up, the quicker we can effortlessly and easily allow it not to impact our balance. If the thought appears "hollow" and we recognize it, we will know it needs urgent attention, and can unmask it, taking away its power over our concentration.

Remember, all thought appears in the field as neutral. How we respond, determines what it will turn into.

We regulate our own reality, so we can potentially create new possibilities, rather than remain in a usual state of duress. In fact, the more we see how predictable our thoughts are—or usual and ordinary and *oh, here it comes again, another thought about X!*—the more we can smile and see we're on repeat and overcome it, so we don't have to keep ruminating the same ideas.

We can then become aware of cycles. Thoughts will come around again on subjects we feel unaffected by, only to find we're triggered by or fixated on them again. But we can very gently let them pass, and move on. We can simply *not* take part in the ruminating, especially when it's repeating. Sometimes when thoughts are in the outlying region, you might even say, *Hmm, I haven't thought about that in ages*—and, simply put, *good!* Don't! But if you do keep thinking on it, it's like calling the thief on the mountain and inviting them to your doorstep!

It's easy (and recognizable) to do this with people: a person we haven't thought of or seen in *years* will appear on the fringe of our perception like a shadow, and we can drag them right into the up-close hollow, and make them ever-present—to a point where we might even physically bring them into our reality and receive a call, or have an "accidental" encounter. *Look who I ran into!*

As you observe the mind, you will recognize it was hardly a coincidence—instead, you gave them your full attention, and since we are all connected to the field of perception, can view their checking-in or appearing, happening simply because *you* thought of them! That goes for all the things you have put aside and then begin to think about again. There isn't any need to pull or cling to anything in your perception range. If you do, you are essentially creating a future with old disturbances.

Keep thoughts in flow and maintain your concentration and attention instead.

The more we are willing to attend to the field of perception in the same way we would sweep a floor—with a gentle *swoosh*—keeping things tidy, the more we can maintain our strength, and the more easily we'll shift perceptions, so that our Inner Sun shines brightly again on the entire territory of the mind.

THE ELEVENTH STEP ON THE HIDDEN PATH TO PEACE AND WHOLENESS

1. Apply the Hidden Path to Peace and Wholeness in whatever way best reveals itself to you in order to establish the Nine (Impartial) Fields of Perception right now.

2. Recognize opportunities, moment to moment, to mix up the way you perceive thoughts around you. As you sense a thought above or to the side, or up-close, or far-away, notice the strength it has, or how it will vie for your attention or centered awareness.

3. Notice moments throughout the day where you are able to anticipate your thoughts and then your emotions, based on where they showed up in your field of perception. Be willing to go easy, if you are repeating and habitually pondering/being distracted by the same things; likewise, be just as easy when you are not.

The Nine (Impartial) Fields of Perception is the eleventh step on the Hidden Path to Peace and Wholeness. The more you can identify the ways that thoughts appear—and utilize them with the knowledge from Chapter 10—the more likely it is you will begin seeing the "true" nature of things. You will be less fooled by your own thinking, freeing your awareness to rest in its natural state of harmony.

Ruminations: The Nine (Impartial) Fields of Perceptions

"Courage to assert a strong will over the senses and emotions is the highest principle of awareness."

– Chapter 11

- -

1. Explain (or draw) where you sense the following types of thoughts arise: (a) *scattered*; (b) *non-resistant*; (c) *the few unseat the many*. Which ones present as easy to sense and which might be more difficult?

- -

2. Explain (or draw) where you sense the following types of thoughts arise: (d) *vast, without need of retreat*; (e) *crisscrossing*; (f) *protracted*. Which ones present as easy to sense and which might be more difficult?

- -

3. Explain (or draw) where you sense the following types of thoughts arise: (g) *obtrusive*; (h) *encircling*; (i) *hollowed*. Which ones present as easy to sense and which might be more difficult?

- -

4. Write down the prevailing thoughts/ideas/images that you are experiencing today and try to describe where you think they appear in the field of perception.

5. Think of a time when a thought-stream seemed to *surround you* and there was no way around or through it. What was it about and how did you overcome it?

6. Think of a time when you experienced a thought that was very *narrow*, really tight and up-close (in the field of perception). There was no way to look past it, but you had to deal with it. What was it about and how did you succeed?

7. Share a time you experienced your mind *crisscrossing* your field of perception. What was it about and how did you gain victory over it?

8. Share a time when your mind was *scattered all over* your field of perception. What was it about and how did you overcome it?

9. Do you perceive your thoughts as mostly disruptive or neutral? How easy/difficult is it for you to return your concentration to centered-attention?

10. Do you believe it's possible to have a quiet mind: *all of the time* or *some of the time* or *rarely*? Explain why.

11. Have you noticed that thoughts appear in cycles? If so, give an example. If not, see if you can identify a thought-stream that reoccurs over hours, months, days/weeks, or even years.

12. When a reoccurring thought keeps reappearing in your field of perception to usurp your concentration, how likely are you to believe that you can never have that thought again? What measures can you take to be free of it?

12

THE WHOLEHEARTED WILL

1. Sun Tzu said: there are five ways of exacting your Wholehearted Will[1] in the Nine (Impartial) Fields of Perception for equanimity to unfold:

    a.   By "cutting off" an encamped thought as soon as it appears exactly at the point of entry in one of the Nine (Impartial) Fields of Perception.

    b.   By "cutting off" the provisions of thought (attention), so it cannot take further root.

    c.   By "cutting off" the vehicles of thought (senses) before they are given the chance to multiply and entangle through the field of perception.

    d.   By "cutting off" the weapons of thought (emotions), so they cannot resupply the field of perception with more distraction.

    e.   By "cutting off" the company of thought so that it cannot groove-in across space and time (eternal eternity), creating cycles of endless habituations to unseat concentration.

2–4. For the Wholehearted Will to establish equanimity, it must be strong and have established a routine of asserting itself over limitations through "tests" that essentially cycle-out the patterns and influences, thereby strengthening the will to embody the courage to succeed. Even if it were to face great difficulty in changing a long-seated pattern (company of thought), it would leap, in an effort to try, and in so doing, establish a routine of success that naturally makes intuition stronger.

---

1   Wholehearted Will can be interpreted as volition paired with true devotion.

5. When the Observer asserts the Wholehearted Will, there are five possible developments you should be prepared for:

6. (a) Thoughts "break out" in the field of attention, so address them at once.

7. (b) Thoughts appear but remain neutral, so remain vigilant, but don't engage.

8. (c) The will overcomes the initial limitation, so maintain your presence if possible.

9. (d) You see a way to assert your will first, rather than waiting for disorder to weaken your resolve.

10. (e) You assert your will, and limitations retreat, but be prepared for them to return and "fight desperately" to regain a foothold and prevent your success.

11. A Wholehearted Will can overcome a limitation for good, but a half-hearted will can hardly expect to conquer a well-grooved habit without it reoccurring.

12. When establishing a presence of unfolding equanimity, you must know the five developments of the will through the cycles of overcoming limitation, which will reoccur if not handled with sheer volition.

13–14. Those who use the Wholehearted Will, as an aid in unfolding equanimity, apply intelligence. The will must be stalwart and unflinching in its ability to unseat limitations and long-held habituated patterns, or it can be robbed of its belief and descend into doubt.

15. Unhappy is the fate of those who try to establish order/harmony without cultivating the spirit of initiative. Without it, it's a waste of time because your effort will stagnate.

16. Hence the saying: *The enlightened Observer lays their plans ahead, while the established concentration cultivates awareness.*

17. Don't move unless you see an advantage; don't use your will unless there is something to be gained; don't engage unless the position is critical.

18. No Observer should engage their will to show off or out of pride/ arrogance.

19. If it is to your advantage to assert your will, then do so; if not, maintain your contemplative focus.

20–21. In time, even when anger or vexation arises, you will recognize an inward state of naturally generated calm and happiness (equanimity), and know you've overcome an aspect of your Self, which will not return.

22. Hence the enlightened Observer is heedful not to allow senses/thoughts to restrict the will, allowing equanimity to unfold as its natural state, thereby, always creating a harmonious, peaceful state of awareness.

INTERPRETING THE LIVING WISDOM OF SUN TZU

Sun Tzu provides a useful tool to navigate our mental battlefield—our fields of perception—and rather than use aggression or resistance, we have at our disposal the Wholehearted Will. We can look at the Wholehearted Will as our unstoppable devotion, a "fire" that signifies our ability to burn up thoughts and mentally perceived obstructions that seem to keep our Inner Sun from shining in flow and balance (Wholeness).

When we employ our Wholehearted Will, we "burn up" the things that we would normally perceive as obstructing our field of vision to see the nature of the world clearly (like the phoenix reemerging from the flame). In simple words, the field of perception is free of thoughts/concepts and a freedom of silence/quiet remains as the ultimate reality.

LESSON ONE (1–10): "CUTTING OFF" DISTRACTIONS AND CHANGING YOUR THINKING

Traveling the Hidden Path to Peace and Wholeness, Sun Tzu is giving us the opportunity to set ourselves free—to reorder the way we've waged war in the battlefield of the mind, our whole lives, in favor of discovering new methods, which will free our field of judgment, worry, fear, competition, doubt, hate— or even high mental states of bliss that seesaw to depression. There is a way forward that embodies serenity, joy, balance, as a ladder to Wholeness.

As we engage the Nine (Impartial) Fields of Perception, we can employ the five ways our Wholehearted Will can bring about (or welcome) equanimity, as a natural and normally occurring state of reality.

To do so, we can recognize the way we can use our will to "cut off" an encamped thought as soon as it appears; we can use the power of our will to "cut off" the provisions of thought (distraction), so it cannot take further root; we can also use our powerful will to "cut off" the senses and emotions before they are given the chance to multiply and entangle our field of perception.

Lastly, we can recognize the way our will can be asserted to "cut off" what seems like a whole army of thoughts grooving-in and limiting our conscious expansion across space and time, creating cycles of endless habituations to unseat concentration.

As we apply our whole heart—our devotion—rather than being harsh and resisting, we can usher in the beauty at our center, which is and always will be joyful and patient. We may experience cycles that feel like "tests," that help us to "cycle-out the patterns and influences," and in turn, if we're attentive and don't give in to our usual habits, we can see change and have more courage to keep going.

It's a process: our intuition is always there, but as we regulate our field of perception, we trust it more, which in turn, unfolds our courage and determination to grow and endure. We don't just take our thoughts as truth anymore; we question them, and then we break them up, and their hold. Success is more possible.

In addition, Sun Tzu lets us know what to plan for when we start to break the hold of our *usual* thinking and change to *new* thinking. With certainty and devotion, we can create a strategy to gain the advantage over the five possible developments: thoughts that break out quickly and should be addressed right away; thoughts that appear but seem harmless—we need to be vigilant, exerting our will, so they don't gain ground and pull our concentration. We also have to keep our will strong once we *have* neutralized a limitation, because it will come around again, to test us or just simply vie for our attention.

We should never wait for our thoughts to weaken our resolve, but learn to assert concentrated attention to overcome them. It takes really listening to, and hearing, what we repeat, as we often do so automatically, or react through deep-rooted habits in our subconscious. If we can notice, and apply our Wholehearted Will, which is fueled by our devotion, the thought or limitation will retreat—or as Sun Tzu puts it, they "break up." We need to remain vigilant, as we may believe we've overcome them, only to see the thought-pattern return and unseat our focus. In short, let nothing—no thought, belief, action, person, tradition, public opinion, etc.—deter you from overcoming your limitations.

LESSON TWO (11–22): BEGINNING TO SEE CHANGES
Our Wholehearted Will can overcome anything. We are (currently) raised to perceive duality, and when we regulate those ideas and question them, or don't go along with it, we give ourselves room to see in another way. We can start small, checking in with the way we think and how our thoughts limit us. Whatever limiting-view or thought we have, we can overcome it. The material world is shaped by our thoughts, and we need not believe what we have always believed without question. The more we apply our will, even half-heartedly, we will begin to see changes.

Ultimately, on our Path to Peace and Wholeness, it takes attuning to our courageous will, with devotion, *whole-heartedly,* to truly conquer those habits that have tricked us over a lifetime and keep them from reoccurring. If we do, Sun Tzu shows us that our consciousness will expand, as it becomes united with the Whole. The more we engage the five developments of the Wholehearted Will, know them, and work through our own cycles, the more we will develop an unshakable stronghold for maintaining serenity.

Once we see even a small change, we will be encouraged to do more, and not be deterred when we (perceive) failure or experience setbacks. We have been working to break up those habits, winning more freedom for ourselves. We use intelligence to "know" ourselves, to be stalwart and unflinching like an army at war, to unseat those long-held habituated thoughts and patterns, so we can "rob" it of its belief.

Furthermore, Sun Tzu shows us that through initiative, we can overcome the feeling of burden that might fool us to think we have "worked hard" or "hard enough." Instead, we push on, not allowing stagnation to eclipse our effort. Rather, we begin to see we can do more and more, effortlessly, our energy unlimited; our strong devotion makes it so we can do *even more* than we thought usual, quicker.

As we become concentrated and unlimited, we see an innate love for what we can do, which permeates into our actions, so we no longer see life as a chore; or work as a burden; or separated into a work-life and a play-life; or a spiritual one versus a non-spiritual one; or a traumatic past and a happy present. Instead, we recognize life as one cohesive whole, echoing with serenity in all actions and directions. Mundane work becomes another chance to show up as your dynamic, boundless Self.

That's why Sun Tzu says, "*The enlightened Observer lays their plans ahead, while the established concentration cultivates awareness.*" Our will makes the future we always dreamed (or have always sensed) possible; even though we've gone years living our life one way, we can, in the next moment, make a new determination, supported by our devotion and will, and live it anew. We do it by overcoming the set-beliefs once holding us back.

Ultimately, we assert our Wholehearted Will a step at a time and gradually we trust in our intuition (Inner Sun), which we can hear and are connected with. We no longer have to listen to the inner complaints and dual-thinking limitations, so each day grows as a harmonious, peaceful state of awareness, *always*.

THE WHOLEHEARTED WAY OF LIVING

Once we begin to employ our will and devotion strategically and wholeheartedly, we can begin to "win" battles over our habituated mind that is regularly anticipating our next move before we actually do it. For example, when you get into your car, you will start it without thinking, because the body predicts what usually comes next, and does it. It would be the same if a person who gave up coffee went to a café—in the same circumstances and environment, their body will sense and operate as it had always done and most likely order a coffee, even if it's been a while since they last had one.

To overcome the programming, it takes great will. It takes volition to recognize your habits, what is limiting you, and overcome it. It takes vigilance and constant review. The "trickiness" of habits and thought-perceptions are long-held—including from childhood responses, the past (or past lives), so we often respond and react how we've always done—and *keep* doing so. We accept the emotion or sense as usual and normal. For example, if you wake up to the sound of thunder and feel scared because you always have, then you will accept it again and again. It takes investigating the sense of fear and why it's there to rid yourself of it. Whether we are children or adults, our fear or phobias started somewhere. We seem programmed to continue to have the same reactions, but that's not necessarily true; according to Sun Tzu, we can change how we think and respond.

Hot and cold are two other forms of duality that can be missed or are accepted as routine and normal. Or take hungry and full—blissful or happy states can be seen as "better than" one that feels like failure or difficulty. If we never question our likes and dislikes, then when we encounter them, they become repetitive reactions or responses. But we can stop resisting and be curious about why we ever started to feel that way in the first place. Perhaps there is an experience tied to them that we can gently overcome, or revise and reinterpret to make a new outcome for ourselves, rather than one essentially automated.

When we observe the seesaw of our mind dictating a sense of *one or the other*, we can see we're not the Master Sun but the prisoner swinging hot, then cold, hotter and cold again: either can be brought to gentle, mental balance to not be controlled by it. When it seems really tough to mentally get free of a thought-stream, we employ Sun Tzu's strategies, including investigation and calculation, and at the very least, acknowledge being alive to experience the "difficulty," in order to restore some balance, through appreciation of one's experience, as a means to divert the idea from taking further hold.

Our Wholehearted Will is the means to take back our mind, body, and spirit, and bring it under the control of intuition, to get off the imbalance of the dual mind and be in accord with our surroundings. We can start with whatever is pulling us *right now*. To start, Sun Tzu says that even acting half-heartedly is better than our awareness being swept away.

As we regulate our field of perception, sensing thoughts and overcoming interruptions, we will experience levels of happiness, or true devotion, as an ordinary state. What can happen here is once we get "there" (experience bliss or a sense of super happiness), we risk "falling" from it; we might check to see what we did wrong, or how we let our bliss go. Equanimity is a constant state of calm, so even extreme bliss brings a false sense of an experience that is deemed "better," and worse, it might even become addictive. This is not to be confused with harmony or serenity; as you experience your Inner Sun, you will recognize the difference.

The key is to see that there is an emotional state swinging back and forth from emotional states, which is only a perception. Even worse is thinking that if you experience anger, or disappointment, etc., you've failed or descended. It too is just another emotional state. When experiencing any emotion, try also to tune in to your intuition, which operates during perceived difficulty, and realize that what you think is a failure is nothing more than your own perceptions changing and dictating the experience, versus the Inner Sun's wisdom of Constant-Awareness and harmony.

Our Wholehearted Will gives us the courage to take new roads toward balance. We can use it to "burn away" the thoughts—and more especially, the thought-streams, those long coils of concepts that we've held onto for a lifetime or longer! As we investigate and maintain our will, we can overcome even the most rooted ones. We can identify the cycles, and when something (figuratively) rears its head again to win our attention, we don't give in.

Those are the times we can say, "not again" or "no more," and be done with it. When we do this, it goes. It can take the cycle of many months to uproot grooved patterns and ideas, or things getting in our way. Even when we are vigilant, things can still seem to be "testing" us to see if we have truly changed a habit. With our intuition acting as teacher, we will welcome *any* experiences that bring us closer to (mental) freedom.

Gradually, we come to acknowledge those precious difficulties as gifts to break down long-held perceptions, and when we succeed, we grow thankful for the disruption that pulled us from our place of calm. We should apply our will and devotion a little at a time, even when we know we might fail, and even if we are sure we *won't* succeed. We must always get up and try again: that is Wholehearted Will.

Use the five developments to overcome the mind's cycles and limitations. Sun Tzu tells us, "The will must be stalwart and unflinching in its ability to unseat limitations and long-held habituated patterns, or it can be robbed of its belief and descend into doubt." It takes initiative and planning, as well as vigilance, to keep going, to assess and find new ways to be. If we are having some success, there's no need to boast or we will find ourselves encountering what we thought we'd already overcome and mastered once more!

With a continued effort, you will see and experience calm-serenity more often, and notice disturbances right away, allowing them to come and go as merely things that you don't need to give power to. And if you do, you will recognize them as helping you to a greater understanding of yourself, always with the goal of being closer to your intuition and Inner Sun (Wholeness).

You can start now, effortlessly.

THE TWELFTH STEP ON THE HIDDEN PATH TO PEACE AND WHOLENESS

1.   *Apply the Hidden Path to Peace and Wholeness in whatever way best reveals itself to you to establish your Wholehearted Will right now.*

2.   *Recognize opportunities, moment to moment, to challenge your weakness/limitations and assure yourself you can create the life you want. Be unpredictable and courageous. Make a list of what has been holding you back and think anew. Follow your inherent dream/purpose. Develop your will and devotion with your whole heart, and let a newfound initiative and courage flood your life.*

3.   *Notice moments throughout the day when you are repeating limitations and assert your will. Watch for cycles and old patterns to reemerge (even months, decades later) after evicting them. Mix up and change your environment, so as to encourage change. Find new ways to see the world without a seesaw-view.*

The Wholehearted Will is the twelfth step on the Hidden Path to Peace and Wholeness. The more you can know the five ways of exacting your will and the five developments that are most likely to emerge, the better you can plan for setbacks and move ahead. Intuition is the inner teacher, the Inner Sun, to guide you, until you can recognize your own oneness, powered by your Inner Sun.

Ruminations: The Wholehearted Will

"Unhappy is the fate of those who try to establish order/harmony without cultivating the spirit of initiative."

– Chapter 12

---

1. Looking at the five ways to apply your Wholehearted Will in the Nine (Impartial) Fields of Perception to bring the mind into balance, which one calls to you most right now, and why?

---

2. Looking at the five ways to apply your Wholehearted Will in the Nine (Impartial) Fields of Perception to bring the mind into balance, which one seems most difficult to apply right now, and why?

---

3. What thought-cycles can you identify as the strongest over the last year, dominating your life? What about over the last five years or more? In what ways have these dominating thoughts/influences created your perception and life? And what strategies can you apply to assert your Wholehearted Will to uproot their hold (to break routines, mindsets, etc.)?

---

4. In asserting the Wholehearted Will, the Observer should be prepared for five possible developments. Of these, which one applies to you most right now, and why?

5. Take a moment to observe your mind and then gently assert your will. Do you notice thoughts returning to "fight desperately" and regain a foothold, preventing your success? What strategy will you undertake to ensure you maintain your focused attention?

6. How can you immediately apply your Wholehearted Will to your life to unseat limitations and long-held habituated patterns?

7. Share an example of where you showed the spirit of initiative or devotion to bring your life/mind into a state of harmony. In what ways can you apply initiative or devotion in your life now?

8. How can you apply the following Inspired Wisdom to your day-to-day life? *"The enlightened Observer lays their plans ahead, while the established concentration cultivates awareness."*

9. Share a time when you overcame something, boasted about it, even in a gentle way, and then it showed up again, and seemed to test you.

10. Share a time when you exerted your will to win the advantage over a habit or a limited way of thinking. What were the results?

11. Share an example of when you experienced anger/irritation and were able to maintain a natural state of equanimity. If you have yet to experience this, what strategies could you apply to do so next time?

12. Describe a time when you experienced equanimity or serenity. Did you experience a sense of loss afterward through the appearance of difficulty? If so, how might you come to realize you remained the same and simply perceived the experiences as different?

13

DISCERNING FRAILTY

1. Sun Tzu said: the Nine (Impartial) Fields of Perception (when) unchecked unfold to create the Ten Thousand Thoughts (things) that appear as the material world, and as such, can establish a patterned cycle of (perceived) difficulties (and duality), to unravel/uncoil (heal/overcome) over (perceived) time/lifetimes. Through regular discernment, the Observer overcomes ordinary perception through the use of the Wholehearted Will, which in turn creates shifts in awareness, so that several hundred thousands of thoughts (habits/ideas/limitations) will vacate, while as many more will be impeded from causing their usual disorder in your seated harmony of awareness.

2. The two sides—unregulated thoughts and Concentrated-Awareness—may (figuratively) face each other for years, striving for a victory, but the realization of Wholeness can be decided instantly, in a single day. This being so, to remain in ignorance about the nature of the enemy-of-thought simply because of discontentment (through perceiving duality), will mean misery for the Whole.

3. The true aim/object of war is to establish peace—and so is it with the war of the mind. Established through observation, the aim is the cessation of conflict within the field of reality, unfolding instead as *genuine unity* with all phenomena. Thus, one who acts in ignorance and in conflict with the world (all reality) is no leader, nor any help to their own (inner) ruler (intuitive Self), nor master of victory.

4. And so, what enables the wise Master Sun to achieve a state of equanimity, accord, harmony, beyond the reach of ordinary consciousness is *foreknowledge.*

5. This is not the foreknowledge akin to premonition; nor can it be deduced through experience (or intelligent reasoning), nor by any deductive calculation.

6. Knowledge of the *truest* nature of the material world (unfolding thoughts/concepts) can only be obtained by observing the *truest* nature of reality *directly*, to see exactly what is unfolding, without aggression, without an Observer who is separated from the experience of the things it perceives.

7. Hence the realization of *discerning frailty*. There are five stages to discerning frailty of all matter/phenomena: *local; inward; as it changes form; as it disintegrates; and extinction or what remains.*

8. When the five stages of discerning frailty (in ordinary phenomena) are employed, it is the way that the true nature of things reveals itself to you, giving you an understanding or unification with the Great Mystery, the thread of life that exists in everything, *everywhere.* Each thing observed is left open just a little bit, like a door about to shut that is stopped, leaving a gap, a pinprick, a space between, through which to observe unrestricted, to *know: what appears harmful also possesses frailty, therefore it too is vulnerable*; it too is changing; it too will perish and fall away. This awareness is the Self's most precious faculty.

9. Employing discerning frailty to your local environment (e.g., your everyday thoughts, actions, people, places, whatever you encounter) is the first stage.

10. Employing discerning frailty to your inward environment (e.g., your inward thoughts, inward perceptions, emotions, senses), is the second stage.

11. Gradually, whether perceiving inward or outward reality, discerning frailty will change form, converting your understanding of the world, granting you a new freedom and mastery that unfolds as tenderness and gentle action. This is the third stage.

12. To this end, the material world of dual reality finally reveals itself, disintegrating your view of separation. This is the fourth stage.

13. Finally, in the fifth stage, the only vision that "survives" is a united, delicate world, one you are no longer separate from, but fully aware of as whole, as you recognize its truest nature as one.

14. Hence in the whole army of awareness, none is more important than discerning frailty. The ability to recognize the delicacy of "all things," is the greatest reward, for it ends the war you've been led to fight, and establishes and advocates an astute tenderness and gentleness toward the whole of existence.

15. Frailty cannot emerge without a certain intuitive, mental discernment and good judgment.

16. It cannot be properly managed without benevolence (kindheartedness) and straightforwardness (or simpleness).

17. Without subtle ingenuity of mind, one cannot ascertain the truth of what frailty communicates (or reveals).

18. *Be subtle! Be subtle!* And use your discerning ability to recognize frailty in every kind of matter/affair and activity.

19. If you fail to "see" the secret nature of something uncovered by frailty, it will destroy your efforts to be united with the Whole.

20. Whether we understand it or not, the nature of frailty exists in both the Observer and the Observed, creating empathy and mercy. We then "watch" with committed fealty to *kindness and gentleness* as our new rulers in command.

21. As our awareness of frailty expands, we must seek every opportunity to lure out "difference" and judgment, to house our awareness comfortably in equanimity/unity. Thus the harsh, competitive world becomes converted to one of reciprocal harmony—as it also possesses great frailty, which we are ever in service to its perfection—as we take up the Gentle-Way.

22. It is through the understanding *that both you and what you observe possess frailty* that you can begin to diminish the separation between an inward and an outer (local) division that is in conflict, by finally seeing (accepting) that it is mutually fragile.

23. It is again owing to the knowledge of frailty that we can "destroy" or cause the extinction of a separate, warring reality that was forever misinforming our worldview.

24. Lastly, it is in the aftermath of frailty's influence that we can no longer be ignorant or neglectful but emerge ever-attentive to the true nature of things.

25. The end and aim of frailty, through all the five stages, is knowledge of the truest nature of the "enemy-of-thought" in the field of perception; and this knowledge can only be derived when we transform our concrete/changeless world into one that is delicate. Hence, employ your ability to perceive frailty in all matters.

26. In ancient times it was said, "Just as water transports a boat safely into harbor, so can it also sink it." So is it with frailty, which will both carry you safely into the true nature of things and also cause its destruction.

27. Hence it is only the enlightened ruler—the Master Sun—who will use the highest intelligence to discern the frailty in all things, and thereby achieve Wholeness, harmony, unity, and peace in all its kingdoms. It is written and said: a war of the mind without discerning frailty is like a person without ears or eyes.

INTERPRETING THE LIVING WISDOM OF SUN TZU

As we observe the *truest* nature of reality—*things,* whatever we see and engage as "the world"—we have a small gap, a space between, through which to view it. Sun Tzu explains that all phenomena have this "space between." It's like a secret passage, a way in and out of each other's territory, much like one a spy would use. And just as a spy will go and gather information on the vulnerability of an enemy, so too you can tap into this pinprick to see the frailty of whatever you are observing. The space between can be used reciprocally for you to know "it" and for "it" to know you.[1]

It's like a door about to close that is stopped from closing. It is symbolized and most easily recognizable in the two small circles (one white, one black) reflected in the Yin and Yang emblem, which signifies that each contains a bit of the other. Sun Tzu is suggesting that if you truly observe something's truest nature, you will uncover its frailty—and when you uncover it in something outside yourself, you will eventually recognize it is the same in you, demonstrating the interconnectedness of all things.

When either side look or perceive each other, they see the usual thing, at face value, but this side-door, this crease in consciousness, has a way of showing the vulnerability of everything:

- A mosquito that bites you is viewed from your point of view as negative or aggressive, but it is vulnerable because of its need; it can be killed or left unfed, yet it is its natural state, and we can experience its effort through the open gap with empathy for its frailty.

- A person who commits a crime against another is also vulnerable, not only because they are human and will perish, but because they cannot see past their own ignorance that they are interconnected with whoever they've hurt.

- A piece of trash appears to be ruinous to an environment, but it too exhibits frailty and deterioration. Likewise, the one who left it there (knowingly/unknowingly) also exhibits frailty, because they are unable to see the interconnectedness of all things.

---

1   While the main focus, or use of this gap, is to recognize frailty, it should be mentioned, the Observed can also use it to observe you. This is why as you enter Concentrated-Awareness you can be easily drawn back, unseated, as old thoughts, habits, ideas, people, that you may've once rooted out, isolated and overcome, can (figuratively) open that "gap," and return, thereby unseating your concentration. Knowing this, then, in the vault of the mind's concentrated attention, the student must guard this "door" or risks invasion.

- Our loved ones who might harm us—the people we encounter daily—mostly live as taught by previous generations or through societal conditioning. This means many are constantly imitating things they see, hear, and learn, recreating established habits or cycles of limitation. But they are no less frail for lacking an understanding of how harm to one is to harm all.

- A volcano is frail as it does what is most natural in a most beautiful way, and then it stops. It is only when we view it as an obstacle, one of destruction, that it becomes our enemy, putting us out of accord with our interconnection to it.

LESSON ONE (1–7): RECOGNIZING FRAILTY

Sun Tzu explains there are five stages of shaking up our field of perception to "see" (or experience) frailty. Once we have burned away our thoughts or the cycles permeating our field of perception, we're given this new view, but can still remain in duality, sensing the changes in things as aggressive and destructive when they're not. Instead, we can welcome peace, as we usher in a cessation of conflict with *everything* and see what is genuinely unfolding.

This foreknowledge of the way things *are,* allows us to become the victor who is no longer separate from the things we perceive. Once we embrace the realization of discerning frailty, we can then employ it in our environments (locally, inwardly, etc.), and as we do, it begins to change the way form appears to us. We become less judgmental, more patient; we begin to see situations with new eyes and with deeper empathy. Things break down, as we are no longer at odds with the world or ourself or others.

As you negotiate forms in your outer world, you'll gradually make the connection inwardly as the forms change more and lose their certainty. (This is because what you observe shares the same frailty as the Observer.)[2] A gradual disintegration takes place. You might visit someone you would normally argue with and find you can't anymore, because the truth of frailty is too strong, causing the world as you knew it to break apart. And the aftermath is union or equanimity.

In this process of re-living the world through the eyes and understanding of frailty, the simplest thing will give you cause to weep, once you have recognized its tender beauty. This is why Sun Tzu says we must learn this

---

2   It goes without saying that the Observer views the Inner Sun (Observed) through the "gap" or "door" left open, recognizing its likeness as One or Wholeness. In other traditions it is a tunnel perceived as the eternal (third) eye opens.

from that which we are observing—especially our circuitous thoughts, which regulate and create the next moment. For as soon as we discover the thread of frailty running through everything, the whole world will take on new meaning: the changeless becomes changing; the hostile contains gentleness; good and bad coexist simultaneously in perfect order and rhythm.

Then when we reveal *our own frailty*, we see how we have been a player in all our own suffering and the suffering of others. *We step out of the army of ignorance and see with gentle eyes how simple and fragile the world is and we won't want to do or cause anything that would ever harm it.*

LESSON TWO (8–14): DEVELOPING EMPATHY AND KINDNESS

Sun Tzu offers the five stages or changes that will take place in your field of perception to uncover the frailty in all matter. It begins with the knowledge that what you perceive one way, also contains another way—whatever the duality you possess toward something, it also contains a thread of something else.

You can begin to try it out in your ordinary local/outward reality and then begin to apply the same inwardly. When you see an angry person acting from limitation, you will discern your own limitation. When you see a person gripped by a habit, you will discern your own habits. This knowledge, Sun Tzu says, is our greatest faculty. You can look at anything and find its thread of frailty and empathize, for you are also just like it: *delicately beautiful.*

Gradually, through your experiences, the sense of duality erodes until it disintegrates, along with your usual perception of reality. You'll experience a sense of oneness and Wholeness, which evolves into a final state where your sense of duality, your separateness to the Whole, will perish and fall away too, ushering in a new freedom that becomes a *walk of serenity.*

St. Teresa of Avila describes it as a state of tranquility and noiselessness. But she also says it's not that you are suddenly without "sin" or disturbances, but that they no longer have the same effect, as there is no fear, no selfish gain, but rather an urgent desire to serve and perform your duty with reverence and devotion.[3]

In so many words, we recognize that each movement, each action, each word or thought, the way we act, *all have the power to impact others*. And as we recognize everyone and everything with frailty, we begin to develop a presence of gentle kindness—a deep caring for all things.

Equally, we are no longer the oppressed, because we recognize we cannot be harmed by the ones who lack an understanding of their own

---

3   Seventh Mansion, Chapter 2, *The Interior Castle.*

frailty. This is why out of the whole arsenal of tools/teaching or wisdom that Sun Tzu offers, we have no greater aspiration than to embrace our ability to discern frailty as the nature of existence.

LESSON THREE (15–26): SEEING WITH NEW EYES

Sun Tzu says very clearly that frailty can't emerge unless you are utilizing "certain intuitive, mental discernment and good judgment." As we've been undertaking strategies to discern the nature of our thoughts and have been scouting the field of perception regularly, we will no doubt begin to possess a new outlook on our lives and environments.

Our new eyes, our new speech, our new actions, will be direct extensions of *benevolence* (kindheartedness) and straightforwardness (simplicity), or effortless tenderness in each moment we live. Without this "subtle ingenuity of mind," we may not see the way frailty communicates (or reveals) itself. We may still be too busy affirming the way things always are. In so many words, Sun Tzu gently reminds us, *"Be subtle! Be subtle!"* Echoing the words of Confucius, who stated that life is very simple, but we are very apt to complicate it.

As we discern frailty in every moment, in every kind of matter/affair and activity, the threads expand and we discern the "secret nature" of things, which is simple, gentle, delicate, effortlessly unfolding and united with the Whole. We go from feeling separate, as a Self that is watching, to recognizing that frailty exists in both the Observer and the Observed, which brings forth our superpowers of keen empathy and mercy.

We then can only be dedicated to kindness and gentleness, and walk in communion and cohesion with others. We will very naturally expand and eliminate our sense of difference. Our harshness and competitiveness with the world transforms into a path of harmony, as we take up the Gentle-Way. Henceforth, everything becomes our teacher, which we humbly bow to and are grateful for.

In the aftermath of frailty's influence, we can no longer accept being ignorant or neglectful of others—we have new eyes to see the true nature of things, which is and will only ever be cooperative. Sun Tzu says, "The end and aim of frailty, through all the five stages, is knowledge of the truest nature of the 'enemy-of-thought' in the field of perception; and this knowledge can only be derived when we transform our concrete/changeless world into one that is delicate. Hence employ your ability to perceive frailty in all matters."

It becomes our lifeline, our magnifying glass, our walk.

A great treasure, this ability to "see" becomes the thing that allows us to witness the true nature of our world clearly for the first time.

LESSON FOUR (27): DISCOVERING PEACE AND WHOLENESS

The entire message of Sun Tzu's wisdom is contained here in these precious words:

> *"Hence it is only the enlightened ruler—the Master Sun—who will use the highest intelligence to discern the frailty in all things, and thereby achieve Wholeness, harmony, unity, peace in all its kingdoms. Thus it is written and said: a war of the mind without discerning frailty is like a person without ears or eyes."*

To discern frailty in all things is the *highest intelligence*. It's a simple truth and teaching. We can very much see that the teacher who offered this wisdom had lived it and understood the need for it during a time of great outer war (as well as the internal ones causing them). We can see the impact it could have too, if a soldier fighting another soldier could see the frailty in the opponent and "awaken" to their interconnectedness—and maybe many did. (I'd like to believe so.)

At the least, we can recognize the whole of humanity living as individual soldiers at war with other soldiers, waging constant and endless war on the battlefield of our minds. Discern the way to end the war now.

USING FRAILTY TO LIVE THE PATH TO PEACE AND WHOLENESS

Have you ever witnessed suffering? It would be hard to miss, as there are so many moments, great and small, that lend themselves to people witnessing suffering in the world. If you can, cast your thoughts back (or maybe suffering is present in your life right now) and consider a moment when you have witnessed the struggle of another (or any living being). What does it look like and how does it make you feel? What can you learn from it?

To observe suffering is to begin to understand the essence of frailty in each of us. For example, we can look at someone with an illness and believe we're grasping the fullness of frailty, but this is rather obvious. Nevertheless, it's a place to start and see that everything in our world possesses frailty. And through this understanding, we can discern our own and then, carrying it further, we can begin to dismantle our beliefs about others and the world, to the point when we lose our sense of separation.

To be a Master Sun is to recognize this common bond we share with all things.

The gentle Path to Peace and Wholeness is very simple, but it has a key ingredient that is very much missed: self-responsibility. You have to do the work and go the full distance. Sun Tzu is clear in that the shift of perception from separation to the realization of Wholeness can be instant, and "decided in a single day," or in the "twinkling of an eye," as the spiritual hymn "I'll Fly Away" relates. Is it really so difficult to perceive Wholeness? No. But it takes self-effort to responsibly see how we all play a part in our own suffering and that of others.

Anyone who wants to get up tomorrow and experience Wholeness can start today by working on themselves, not someone else. Many blindly or prematurely seek to help and fix others, when in fact, the way to impact change in the world is to actually take the time to change themselves, *first*, and recognize their own cycle of disorder, perpetuating a long history of conflict. Be the humble student, full of devotion for others, while willingly looking at the way you think and act, as a way of life and a lifelong journey. In that way, we can gently come together with others to form a circle of cooperation.

If we can do the work to embody a Master Sun, and the next person does too, and the next, we become a link of suns—like a jeweled thread that can radiate love and light across the globe (and beyond) and especially, the field of perception that makes up our shared reality. Free to grow, we can enter the global stream with our own unique treasure to make peace, unity, cooperation, unconditional love, and harmony, necessary and normal. We have free will to decide what impact we make, and like it or not, though it may seem like we're kind and generous to others, our unregulated thoughts that cleave to worry, fear, doubt, superstition, difference, and duality, are making a future at war.

But we can change that *in the next unfolding moment.*

Sun Tzu's Path to Peace and Wholeness is a call for us today to consider our own gentle steps forward—*the new motto:* leave no trail of disquieted thoughts behind!

We all contribute. And we now have the *foreknowledge* of how to make a difference. Imagine the impact that could be made if everyone committed to working on their own thread of light, their own ideas/thoughts so that they no longer created the same habitual cycles of fear (etc.), but a new flowering of unadulterated (energetic) peace! It's actually already here and happening—and has always been.

Truly.

There is more peace and kindness in the world than not. It coincides with war, and we are, essentially, in any given moment, deciding which one we will choose: peace or war. You have to look to see it, and not accept any helpless, limited view as a permanent reality. And if you believe it is, then change it. We choose where and what we focus on and we can change any situation. It begins with recognizing the underlying current of frailty that everything possesses.

Know this, and what was an enemy or a horror loses its power.

Oneness or Wholeness—our natural evolution of conscious-unity—is the discernment that the most terrible things and people also possess frailty. In the long, jeweled thread, everyone has a seat. It doesn't exclude *that person over there causing a ruckus!* That person, too—there is nothing that does not possess frailty. To begin to see it creates a give-and-exchange, until you only see a single thread running through all life and it stirs you to overwhelming compassion, from which there is no return. It's not special or sacred. On most days you will still be ordinary. But you will no longer experience separation or isolation.

Peace is possible in the next moment, in the next thought and action, in the next smile you give someone rather than hate. It is possible the moment you recognize that frailty exists in you and everyone, and from it give the whole world an embrace. You'll still have difficulties, you'll go to work and eat, and be social, but it will have a different appeal as you recognize how your own actions in each arena might hurt others (and animals, the environment).

No longer will you be thinking of yourself, but the Whole.

Every action, each thought you have, can impact someone, and you would never want to be careless again—in fact, all you'll want to do is ensure no one suffers, for you'll know (intuit) that the Whole suffers. Change will come. You will venture into the world attentive and anticipating the needs of others, giving wholeheartedly in every direction to serve with a sense of cooperation and devotion that is ever-evident in our world.

It is alive and thriving. Know it and put it into gentle action.

We all have an Inner Sun that can recognize the hidden frailty in our greatest "enemies" who are and ever will be one with us. Let the gentle warrior free. Gather up your Wholehearted Will and lay plans to "see" and objectively observe your mind and what it costs you (and others) when it is disordered and without patience and unity; undertake strategies through responsibility to calculate your own nature (let others do the same without your input); root your concentration and begin to see how your perceptions have led to your beliefs and limiting-views; establish Contemplative-Awareness; know the variations of the way thoughts and ideas present in the field of perception; concentrate and allow your consciousness to expand.

Do not give up or retreat.

Do not accept that you have done enough.

Do not ever stop working on your actions, thoughts, emotions, until you "know" the essence of frailty. Without it, you're essentially blind to knowing the Wholeness full of potential and possibility.

That is how we let our Inner Sun shine everywhere.

Arriving, we unfold as a *Master Sun.*

The war to free the mind—*to free the world*—will be won with gentleness.

May the Gentle-Way guide your steps.

May you be victorious.

THE THIRTEENTH STEP ON THE HIDDEN PATH TO PEACE AND WHOLENESS

1. *Apply the Hidden Path to Peace and Wholeness in whatever way best reveals itself to you in order to begin discerning frailty right now.*

2. *Recognize opportunities, moment to moment, to see even the "harshest" people or circumstances as opportunities to uncover the delicate nature beneath the surface. Observe your mind's resistance when regarding people you don't like or situations that are difficult or unredeemable, and discover the "space between," the small gap left open for you to see through with soft eyes.*

3. *Notice moments throughout the day when you're not discerning frailty but acting on habit or old ideas, or going along with whatever the consensus thinks or perceives. Pick a person or a situation that brings difficulty and observe your thoughts for discerning frailty. (Journal them if it helps.) Investigate and free yourself. Find gentleness in the most difficult and defamed situations/people. Then turn and offer it to yourself. Notice the frailty in your own shortcomings and offer empathy instead.*

Discerning Frailty is the thirteenth step on the Hidden Path to Peace and Wholeness. The more you can know the frailty in all things, the more likely your perception of separation will unfold and reveal Wholeness. Let your Inner Sun open wide to include unconditional love for all beings and all things.

May you walk tenderly on the Gentle-Way to self-victory!

Ruminations: Discerning Frailty

"Foreknowledge enables the wise Master Sun to achieve a state of equanimity, accord, harmony, beyond the reach of ordinary consciousness."

– Chapter 13

---

1. When we begin to make changes in our way of thinking, we essentially end thought-streams. Take one thought-stream that is very strong and write about it. What future thoughts can you predict would be eliminated if you were to uproot this thread completely? How might your life change?

---

2. Is it possible for our duality and discontentment, which prevents us from recognizing our oneness/Wholeness with others, to dissipate in a day? Why do you think it usually takes longer? How are the patterns of your own mind that create separation keeping you from experiencing Wholeness?

---

3. How can the *foreknowledge* of frailty assist you in creating ever-lasting peace with others/your world?

---

4. Share your ideas about frailty, what it means and how you have/have not observed it. How might it assist you in "observing the *truest* nature of reality directly"?

5. Of the five stages of frailty, which one(s) have you experienced? What areas have benefited from discerning frailty?

6. Have you ever witnessed suffering? What does it look like and how does it make you feel? What can you learn from it?

7. Sun Tzu explains, "Frailty cannot emerge without a certain intuitive, mental discernment and good judgment." How have you used your intuition to create less separation in your life?

8. We're being asked to "*Be subtle! Be subtle!*" In what ways are you prone to "do something" without necessarily seeing if it's just more of your usual actions—still harsh, less gentle? What strategies can you add to regulate and check yourself?

9. Share a story or experience when you experienced that both you and what you observed possessed frailty—or were in fact similar or equal, perhaps even contrary to a long-held belief?

---

10. In what areas of your life are you actively fostering an unbiased unity, harmony, peace, and perfection? (For example, in cooking, work, hobbies, walking, global community.)

---

11. In what ways can you continue to actively foster an unbiased unity, harmony, peace, and perfection?

---

12. Having taken the journey with Sun Tzu, what is the first thing you will undertake on the Hidden Path to Peace and Wholeness?

AFTERWORD

THE PATH TO PEACE AND
WHOLENESS WITHIN YOU

The teacher is within—but how do we discover what is hidden?

Sun Tzu's complete Path to Peace and Wholeness will guide you to reveal your own hidden truth, your hidden warrior, *as it will take the heart and spirit of a warrior to overcome and trust yourself,* to "hear" and "know" your highest truth. We must choose it; we must be willing to face ourselves and do the work needed. You have this moment to decide which way you will go: whether you will continue to wage more war with yourself, or if you are finally weary of fighting and resolve to end it. All it takes is a small step, a commitment, to begin.

To help you on your way, I've included twelve practical ways to apply the teachings on the Hidden Path to Peace and Wholeness. Each practice is not intended to overshadow Sun Tzu's teachings, but to demonstrate the resources available to us every day that can help engage your concentration and awareness, to grow and expand your perception of your life and the world. When we are active, engaging new paths and ideas, we're more likely to make change, challenge our rooted perceptions and see Wholeness and unity where we might have only ever seen disorder, separation, and difficulty. Most importantly, we're in control of the next moment and by implementing one or all of these practices, we will create harmony in and around our lives.

1. MAKE EVERY DAY A "SUN" DAY

Dedicate a single day to solitude. Go without noise. Create a day where you're unconnected, unavailable, and can be easy with your time and yourself. Allow space to ruminate your life, to consider your dreams and to hear your intuition. You might open your Sun Day with a formal meditation, followed by 3–6 hours of quiet and concentration to awaken your Inner Sun. Or it may be you seek quietude in the natural spaces around you.

Be un-busy and yet willful with your devotion to love yourself, the day, others. In solitude, we can decompress, recharge, and renew. It gives us a sacred time to center our core toward harmony and unity. Allow your Wholehearted Will and intuition to guide the day. Be open and discover what it's like to trust your source. Find ways to carry the peace you gain into the week, and support your effort by turning off the world/technology at a particular time each night.

Soon every day will be a Sun Day!

2. BEGIN A RUMINATION JOURNAL

Begin now to frame your morning and evenings with a journal practice. Each day offers us infinite opportunities to create—be it our dreams or a new future—and yet sometimes, no matter how much we endeavor to make time for it, the hours, days, and weeks can go by and we find instead that we've been led away from our goals.

Undertake the strategy of ruminating your life path through journaling. In doing so, we not only tap into our spacious intuition, but we also create space to be still, in order to nurture investigation into the limitations we'd like to overcome. Start with a daily journaling practice. Journal each morning before rushing off to work or other tasks, and return again at night, after turning off the world, to review the day and make plans for the next.

As you make a commitment to return daily, you'll see your concentration deepen and intuition unfold, especially over the long-term. Utilize your journal to answer the questions in this book and contemplate your setbacks and successes. By journaling, you will gain access to your inner teacher and learn more about yourself as you endeavor along Sun Tzu's Hidden Path to Peace and Wholeness.

3. LEAVE NO THOUGHT-TRAIL BEHIND

Start to engage the world with a soft hand and footprint. Notice when you walk heavily, talk loudly, bang and explode upon your environment. Be mindful of those around you. Each action creates an energetic imprint in the field of perception that is felt around you, by others, knowingly or not.

In its most simplistic form, remember a time when you weren't feeling well and someone made you a bowl of soup or a cup of tea; your felt-sense of comfort came in the vibration of love/order/harmony transported from the maker into the soup and to you. Similarly, if it had been made in a hurry or begrudgingly, you'd have felt it too.

Take action each day to engage your world of actions with tenderness, so much so, that you don't even leave a stray thought behind. When you walk, be mindful of *where* or *what* you're stepping upon—you can actually become aware of the tiniest ant and avoid stepping on it! Notice if you're in a hurry, rushing others around you, and how those movements help create disturbances to others, and make a change. All our actions should include consideration for others. Soon, we begin to see how harsh we have been and can begin to live effortlessly without leaving even a stray emotion behind as we go!

4. SET THE TABLE

Each day make time to "set the table" for another person or living being in some capacity—it can be a selfless prayer for global peace; it might be an offering of your time, your mind, your listening. It might be to free all the bugs stuck in the windowsill or to read poetry to your community. It might be holding monthly dinners for your family or those in your community who are most in need. Be still and guided to who or what would most benefit.

When we (figuratively) "set the table" on a daily basis, we're carving space for others and doing so with excellence and care. We make an offering that ensures each plate or napkin is in place, each seat made special—it is through the preparation (of any task for others) that concentration flows, we reach a heightened awareness to ensure all is perfect and harmonious.

In doing so, those receiving our bounty can feel and experience the kindness and wonder we evoked in the process of creation—to essentially experience unity (sometimes for the first time). Devotion is fueled by genuine love (benevolence) and enthusiasm to make others happy. Find inventive ways to "set the table" for all those you come in contact with, perhaps family, friends, and coworkers, and gradually, open that circle to include strangers—keep opening the circle to include all living things!

5. LIVE THE LIFE YOU'VE DREAMED *INSIDE* OUTSIDE

Follow your inherent wisdom, unfolding from your intuition to live your dreams, your goals—the things that come to you to impact and create— *right now*. When we contribute our art, our living wisdom in the world, seen or unseen, we live purposefully and engage our beauty, while offering it selflessly to others to experience. So often, we see others living their dream and feel there is no point, or it's too difficult, or that ours doesn't matter.

But even a song sung in earnest, with no apparent audience, gives off a vibration and can be felt by others, knowingly or not; it will lift the joy in the world. In this way, you can live your life as a hub of light—if you build or invent things or whatever your interest, when you do it with Concentrated-Awareness, the will and your intuition work in unity, and you will carry that experience into everything else you do.

6. FILL THE NEED
No matter where you are in the world, there is a need somewhere that can be filled by your contribution. More often, we may not feel we're the ones to fill it or that someone else will. Give yourself permission to fill needs. Actively take notice of the needs around you that would benefit from change. Don't wait. Do what you can and be open to include others.

Ask yourself, *what one small effort can I contribute today, that will potentially create a big change tomorrow.* Think small and doable, *right now.*

It might be a need somewhere in your home, your neighborhood, your community, or the world-at-large. One small effort today can and will create a big change tomorrow. In the process, as we make a small effort of change, we can begin to see how the world—which often seems firm and unchangeable—can be transformed and impacted through our attention, joy, and gentle-care.

7. RECLAIM AND RECAST YOUR ANCESTRAL TREE
To honor our *new* walk in this place and time, we can collect the long chain of footprints left by our ancestors, which embodies their energetic vibration of emotions. Honor the goodness of your family tree, while also reclaiming the ancestral past that was impacted by hate, war/suffering, violence/hurt to others, and recast it all in love, harmony, union, forgiveness, and peace; this allows for a healing of the collective past to take place, that will free the Earth of the "heavy" vibration that still permeates it.

Spend time ruminating your family's history, the wars they may have fought, the suffering and hardship they may have collectively endured and/or caused, and reclaim it in the name of love and forgiveness. In turn, recast it—to *recast*, means to give something a different form by melting it down and reshaping it. On behalf of all your ancestors, acknowledge the past and recast it with ever-new joy, knowingly taking the next step into the future with awareness of reciprocity and love, that can create unity with all peoples in the next unfolding moment.

Honor their old traditions by recasting them safely and responsibly in today's world (for example, old recipes can be crafted without interfering with the lives of animals or other harmful practices). The more we repeat the process, the greater the energy that is set free, the more you'll see rebirth and rejuvenation the world over.

8. BALANCE YOUR LIVING SPACES

When we dedicate time to bringing balance to our living spaces, we can break up our habituated thinking about ourselves and others. Start now by peacefully organizing your living spaces (for example, in the home, work, or car). Donate usable items not being used. Let go of items that you are energetically connected to and hanging on to from the past: when you free yourself of the past, you make more room for a new you to emerge. Equally, the energy connected to those items gets freed up and you will feel more energetic to begin new projects.

Be efficient and tidy. If your areas of living are a mess, it mirrors your interior world. Make time to clear clutter and embody order, which will carry into your concentration and focus. Minimize and simplify what remains. Once your immediate areas are orderly, begin to look out into the world for areas like your neighborhood, street, parks, and so on, which are routinely littered with rubbish.

As you dedicate time to caring for these areas, you bring your own attention to the matter, and can imbue the work with a vibration of love and harmony—but be mindful, as you collect trash, you can easily begin to judge the people who have intentionally or inadvertently left it. Be kind and loving by spreading understanding as you free natural spaces of garbage. Gradually, as you develop a practice over months or years, these areas will begin to permeate with your love and the rubbish will naturally decrease.

9. GROW A MEADOW

Growing a meadow has many benefits beyond just the beauty it will create in your life and to those who see it. We create a relationship with the Earth and learn to communicate in a new, special way with its elements, soil, plants, and animals. As we watch our meadow grow, we can appreciate the value of the Earth's resources, and the necessity of cooperation locally and globally to sustain an ecosystem.

Whether we realize it or not, as we tend our meadow, we also raise our energetic vibration through physical activity, which in t··· ··store our calm, our serenity, making us even more in tune v ···nt Through the movements of gardening, we becom and harmony as we find our flow. No matter h·

you have to begin your meadow, you can tap into your amazing creativity. Plan time to survey your immediate area to see where you can begin to cultivate trees, flowers, and herbs.

Likewise, you participate in the cycle of life, as bees and bugs will frequent your flowers and create food for birds and other creatures, large and small, and as high as hawks and eagles. Talk and meditate with your meadow; be guided by intuition and offer gratitude every day, and watch it grow! Visit at dawn and dusk, as often as possible, to greet the day with your new garden. Spend time during the day when you can. In doing so, you create a regular practice to regulate your mind to notice the true nature and frailty of all things, while also bringing it into harmony.

10. GRANT DIGNITY TO ALL LIVING THINGS

To live harmlessly in the world is to see our oneness with all living things. On the journey to grow aware and realize our Inner Sun, we recognize the true nature of existence, and that all beings are entitled to be free of suffering. This includes those creatures that have been vilified and feared generationally, like the humble rat, the gentle mosquito, the fierce shark, and the perfumed skunk—each has an honorable purpose and nature to fulfill.

On our journey, we can bring joy and happiness to many living species. We can act kindly toward all life wherever we go, seeing them through eyes of compassion and making room for their happiness. We can honor living beings by observing, without disturbing or hurting—or feeling the need to be rid of them. We can restore dignity to animals, insects, trees, rivers, plants by noticing their needs and providing for them.

We can also rededicate open spaces to wildlife that is free of human activity—including human thinking and energy—it can be a small window-box for flowers, a piece of property, or as big as remediating brownfields for future generations. Equally, we can re-devote our city spaces and rooftops to cultivating new forests, vertical gardens, and inventive natural spaces that include consideration for all living beings.

Begin with a daily affirmation and commitment: *"I will do my best to love all creatures, big and small, and learn ways to protect the lives of all living things in everything I do."*[1] When we live harmoniously with all living creatures, we restore their dignity and freedom, creating a more congruent world, doing no harm wherever we go.

---

[1] For more on the ability to recognize our kind impact on all living beings, see the author's *Kindness for All Living Things.*

11. ONE MEAL A DAY

One of the most immediate ways we can cultivate change in our lives and practice Concentrated-Awareness, while impacting change globally, is through ruminating and renegotiating our relationship with food. With little effort, we can begin to see how interconnected we are with others through our food consumption. We rely on farmers the world over; the weather, planets, and earth, to grow it; and countless other gentle-helpers that support the delivery of food to us.[2]

Likewise, we can begin to grow aware of the portion we're taking, and minimize it, while also becoming mindful of the practices we're supporting that could be harmful to others (people, animals) and the environment, and make adjustments. You might implement a year-long commitment to eating only one meal a day. In doing so, you'll begin to create a rumination practice, as you see the impacts that will include less consumption; less garbage and waste on a weekly/yearly basis; more stamina and energy; reduction in healthcare; more free time, as less is spent in purchasing, preparing, or socializing.

When we gather our focus on one meal, we're more likely to cherish it, to see and taste and honor what we're eating, mindful of how it nourishes our body and mind, while considering all those responsible for providing it for us.

12. PRACTICE RECIPROCITY

Sun Tzu's teachings echo the practice of reciprocity[3] as a way of life. In doing so, it becomes more than an intellectual understanding that *I will treat others with the same respect I want to be treated with.* It goes much deeper and implies: *who I am on the inside is the same as what is on the inside of others*—and if that's true, we can experience and discover for ourselves the delicate thread that connects all people.

Just like when we discern frailty, when we meet others, we can do so with an awareness that *their suffering is our suffering,* felt and experienced the same way; and through empathy—through not wanting suffering for ourselves—we will not want it for another. Thus, we will seek harmony and peace in all our words, actions, and relationships.

---

2   For more on the ability to recognize our interconnectedness with "all" people through food, see the author's book, The *Whole World Inside Nan's Soup* (Yeehoo Press, 2021).

3   shu, 恕

As our understanding of reciprocity increases, so does our empathy. The circle of life expands, as we recognize we're not able to live without those beautiful helpers the world over supporting our life and experience, who we can now honor with our thankfulness, our kindness, our understanding, our patience, and most of all, our self-responsibility that discerns we are the root of others' suffering when we set aside our interconnection.

SUN TZU'S HIDDEN PATH TO PEACE AND WHOLENESS WORKSHOP

with Hunter Liguore

During this one- to three-day workshop, participants will learn how to apply the concepts shared in *The Modern Art of War: Sun Tzu's Hidden Path to Peace and Wholeness* to their life through a series of discussions, written exercises, and direct-observation practices.

The Modern Art of War: Sun Tzu's Hidden Path to Peace and Wholeness presents a new interpretation that deals specifically with creating "gentle" lives in harmony with the world—the "battle" Sun Tzu writes about is the fight for control over the mind and the thoughts that rule it. Participants will learn how to "conquer" the mind through direct experiences, including the wisdom of frailty, specific to Sun Tzu's school. To that end, students will engage the root of conflict (war) that begins "within" to carry it forward in peace.

The Modern Art of War: Sun Tzu's Hidden Path to Peace and Wholeness emphasizes self-knowledge, direct-observation, and inner-trust, so participants can discover their "hidden" teacher or warrior within.

For online or in-person booking, contact: www.hunterliguore.org

ABOUT THE AUTHOR

Hunter Liguore is an award-winning writer, professor, and historian, with a lifelong study in philosophy, specializing in the work of Sun Tzu. She's studied with Nobel Peace Prize Laureate, John Hume (North Ireland), and has undertaken critical research in peace and social justice studies. Her unique writing explores interconnectedness with all people, reciprocal relationships with the natural world, and kindness and empathy for all, without exception. Her other books include *The Whole World Inside Nan's Soup.* She's a writing professor at Lesley University and hosts peace walks in New England. Learn more at: hunterliguore.org